"Me,

An inside lo
Heart of a Self-Absorbed Mother

Linda Mather

Psychotherapist, Trainer & Author

"ME. ME, ME"
An inside look into the fragile heart of a self-absorbed mother

"ME. ME, ME"
An inside look into the fragile heart of a self-absorbed mother

"Mirror, Mirror on the wall, who is the fairest of them all"

An extract from the fairy tale Snow White which demonstrates a good reflection of a narcissistic stepmother.

"ME, ME, ME"
An inside look into the fragile heart of a self-absorbed mother

Linda was born in Easington Colliery, Co Durham in 1958, and then moved to Leicester in the early 1960's, which is where she spent her childhood. But, it was in 'Shakespeare County,' Warwickshire, where she says she 'grew up' during and after completing her counselling diploma.

She is now an experienced Therapist, supervisor, & trainer, behavioral family therapist & author. She has three grown up children and eight grandchildren.

Also by Linda Mather

Novels
A Woman's world
Jane, me and myself
The Haymaker

Self help books:
I shall wear purple
I shall be blue
I shall be clean
Teenagers are from Pluto

Children's Books:
The fairy on top of the Christmas tree
The mystery behind Grandpa's chair
Crystal Magic

Text Books
Introduction to counselling skills and theory
Manual for certificate to Diploma in Therapeutic Counselling

"ME. ME, ME"
An inside look into the fragile heart of a self-absorbed mother

Copyright @ 2015 Linda Mather

This book contains material under International and Federal Copyright Laws and Treaties. Any unauthorised reprint or use of this material is prohibited. No part of this book may be reproduced or transmitted in any form or by any means, electronic or mechanical, including photocopying, recording or by any information storage or retrieval system without express written permission from the author.

ISBN-13: 978-1507748664
ISBN-10: 1507748663

http://lindamather.yolasite.com

Cover art by Dreamstime

All characters in this publication are fictitious and any resemblance to real person's, living or dead, is purely co-incidental

"ME. ME, ME"
An inside look into the fragile heart of a self-absorbed mother

Contents Page

Introduction
1. What is Narcissism?
2. Symptoms of a narcissist mother
3. What made your mother who she is and why can't she empathise?
4. When did you notice your mum was different?
5. Unhealthy behaviours that you may develop & How it affects your relationships
6. All you do for her and still feel unloved, praise with a sting in the tail & I can do better than that
7. Scapegoating versus the golden child versus the black sheep
8. Triangulation, Narcissist supply and gaslighting
9. Projection, silent treatment, hoovering & the flying monkeys
10. Will she change and how might she change - Contact or no contact?
11. The fragile heart
12. Healing your own wound
13. Coming to terms with life with a mum who is different & moving forward
    Epilogue

"ME. ME, ME"
An inside look into the fragile heart of a self-absorbed mother

Introduction

Self absorbed mothers have been part of our society for thousands of years. It has enabled writers to pen fairy tales such as Snow white and Cinderella. The self absorbed characters are usually portrayed as evil step mothers, but biological mothers are just as capable (either in awareness or totally outside their conscious awareness) of abusing and manipulating the minds and hearts of their offspring.

As therapists we are well aware of the 'self absorbed' or narcissistic mother and the impact they have on their children's lives and behaviours which predominantly come out in adulthood. They fill our therapy rooms and keep us in business. Without a doubt they will access therapy at some point in their life usually after several failed relationships or when suffering with anxiety or depression or both. As their story enfolds we learn about the 'hidden' and often covert abuse they have experienced at the hands and minds of the one person, the first person they have learned to trust, the person who gave birth to them and were given the child to nurture and love unconditionally throughout their lives, their mother. The

"ME. ME, ME"
An inside look into the fragile heart of a self-absorbed mother

maternal figure that because of her own inner torment was not able to nurture her children in a healthy way.

We now live in a society where we see mums continuously on their computers playing angry birds, candy crush or networking on facebook or taking 'selfies' to publish on social media. They are on their mobile phones, I pads and laptops and their children are crying for attention. They say "just a minute honey" which is nice words if they were not giving a covert message to their children that "this black box in front of my face is far more important than you or your emotions right now".

Are they all narcissists we may well ask? People who are self absorbed? No I don't think that they are, but what concerns me the most as a therapist and as a mother is 'what about the lack of emotional attachment' that this 'new' behaviour may have on their children, which makes me ask the question are we nurturing children to become narcissists as they develop.

All the theorists will tell us how important emotional attachment to our mother is and without it the impact that this may have on the child's life, both in infancy and in adulthood.

"ME, ME, ME"
An inside look into the fragile heart of a self-absorbed mother

Is this behaviour breeding more and more narcissists? Children that do not have their emotional needs met so therefore are not able to meet the emotional needs of significant others in relationships and just as importantly their own children's?

In this new world of technology it is extremely frightening how distant we are all becoming to our fellow human beings. We communicate by telephone, by social media, by Skype. We splatter our dirty washing all over social network sites watching distractedly for all the 'likes' and getting a quick 'feel good' fix the more that we get.

> FACEBOOK
> Helping narcissists share purposely vague 'Cries for Attention' since 2004!

We meet people via internet dating, avoiding socialising in public places. For goodness sake some will even have cybersex, how intimate is that?

What has happened I wonder to 'contact' to the pleasurable experience of touch, eye contact, active listening, a cup of tea and a good old fashioned chinwag.

"ME. ME, ME"
An inside look into the fragile heart of a self-absorbed mother

As a psychotherapist I am working more and more with clients who have been raised by a narcissistic parent, predominantly in my practice mothers. Client's whose parent couldn't deal with their emotions from a very young age, which resulted in them growing up suppressing their feelings believing that their emotions were unmanageable to others. Clients who believe they are not normal and have never quite felt 'good enough'. Most of those children did not come from the 'technology era' however I envisage that in another twenty years or so we are going to be seeing more and more clients with mental health problems such as depression, anxiety, guilt and grief for the parent that they never felt loved by due to this lack of attachment.

I am fully aware that equally there are narcissistic fathers out there and people in narcissistic relationships that are suffering untold distress. However there seems to be endless books on the market about this but very little about self absorbed mothers and as my experience is working with the children of narcissistic mothers this is what I shall be addressing in this book.

This book has been written to help clients who feel that they may have had a narcissistic parent. It will enable them to gain an understanding of and insight into the heart and mind of a narcissist mother and to develop awareness into the impact that this now has on their relationships in the here and now. It is also a useful resource for therapists to gain further insight into this subject to enable them to work with and support clients that are

"ME. ME, ME"
An inside look into the fragile heart of a self-absorbed mother

presenting in a way that they may have lived through this painful experience.

I hope it achieves this and more and helps each and every one of you to recover and move on into healthy, mature and loving relationships, breaking the cycle of generational narcissism to raise healthy and functional children of your own.

Linda Mather

"ME. ME, ME"
An inside look into the fragile heart of a self-absorbed mother

Chapter One
What is Narcissism?

The word Narcissist came from the Greek mythology. There was a young man named Narcissus who fell in love with his own image reflected in a pool of water. Unable to consummate his love, Narcissus lay gazing into the pool, hour after hour and day after day, ignoring all the beautiful women around him. He finally changed into a flower that bears his name.

Sigmund Freud introduced narcissism in his psychoanalytical theory he suggested that narcissism is actually a normal part of the human psyche. He believed that we are all born without a basic sense of self and as we develop through experience in infancy and early childhood people gain a sense of self. He believed that if we transferred this love of our self onto another person, giving away our love then people would be left with less ability to nurture, protect or defend themselves. This then leaves them with a low self esteem and the need for love, affection and adoration becomes vital.

Narcissistic Personality Disorder is now a classified diagnosis in the diagnostic statistical manual of mental disorders (DSM). The symptom list is as follows:

"ME. ME, ME"
An inside look into the fragile heart of a self-absorbed mother

If the person shows five or more of the symptoms they may well be on the narcissistic spectrum.

1. An exaggerated sense of self importance
2. Preoccupation with fantasies of unlimited success, power, brilliance, beauty, or ideal love
3. Believes they are special and can only be understood by, or associate with, other special or high status people or institutions
4. Requires excessive admiration
5. Has a sense of entitlement
6. Selfishly takes advantage of others to meet their own needs
7. Lacks empathy
8. Is often envious of others or believes others are envious of them
9. Shows arrogant, haughty, patronising or contemptuous behaviours or attitudes

Narcissistic Personality Disorder (NPD) is presented as a person whom is self centred or egotistical in their thinking and behaviour in all or most aspects of their relationships. Their behaviour can cause a lot of emotional distress to others and they very rarely ever admit or take responsibility for their behaviour. It is always someone else's fault.

They exaggerate success stories to attract the attention that they so desperately need and also to impress.

"ME. ME, ME"
An inside look into the fragile heart of a self-absorbed mother

They often tell lies to make their own light shine brighter. They are unable to recognise from other people's speech or actions that they may be disliked, even after they've displayed callous behaviour towards this person.

They have to be the centre of everyone's world. If they are not then this can be extremely painful for them resulting in them reacting in a vindictive and cold-hearted way. They will create dramas in social situations and before family events to attract attention.

They can do the most revengeful things when in this pain that most of us struggle to understand. What we have to remember and I think is an important point to make is that NPD's are in enormous pain most of the time. It is natural for us all when we are in physical or emotional pain to behave in ways which are not healthy. This is why people with NPD behave in destructive and grandiose ways. It is to manage their pain.

They will try in manipulative ways to turn other family members or friends against us and often play the 'victim' to achieve this goal. This is because they need all of the attention to themselves, they need this to survive; drama's appear to make them strive. If you know someone that has narcissistic tendencies you will notice that when there is not a drama in their life they become withdrawn and depressed.

They hate to be challenged about their behaviour, or told that they are not 'perfect'; as they hate to be seen as having any imperfections. If you do challenge them they will exaggerate the argument, behaviour or disagreement to make you look bad, putting their own slant on the incident. They may hurt you in

"ME. ME, ME"
An inside look into the fragile heart of a self-absorbed mother

despicable ways as they need you to feel bad to feel good themselves. Other people's pain and discomfort is like oxygen to them without which they would not survive.

They are exceptionally good at denial. They will have different perceptions of events that have happened in yours and their life. The denial is often centred on things that they feel they have done wrong or feel bad about but couldn't possibly admit.

The most common punishment inflicted by narcissistic parents if they feel wounded, (although not limited to) is the withdrawal of their love. Often clients will say to me "she gives me the silent treatment for years". For some this is respite for others it is painful. It can create a painful wound in the child of rejection or abandonment, which has a huge impact on their childhood, adult life and relationships.

They will discount your feelings in a way that leaves you feeling that your emotions are unmanageable. Such as making comments like "you are over reacting", "you are crying over spilt milk" or they will turn the focus on to their feelings which are of course so much more justified than yours.

They need to be in control of everything and if they lose control then this can lead to bouts of depression. With many narcissists you will never get anything right they will criticize you for everything that you do. This leaves children of narcissist mothers desperately trying to please and desperately trying to get everything right.

Last but not least they have no empathy for you or others. I remember a client telling me the story that her mum had rang

"ME. ME, ME"
An inside look into the fragile heart of a self-absorbed mother

complaining that her friend was no fun anymore and was quite snappy with her. The conversation proceeded as follows:

> **Client:** Well mum she has just gone through a very messy divorce. At her time in life it can't be easy for her. She's not going to be a breath of fresh air right now.
>
> **Mother:** Well I've told her that if she wants to keep our friendship she needs to go to the doctors for anti depressants.

This is a typical demonstration of an NPD's lack of empathy. The focus was on the friend being well enough to meet the mother's needs not the needs of the friend.

A typical example of a narcissistic mother and her relationship with her child is shown in the film 'The Black Swan.' It depicts a mother who tried to live her life through her daughter, although became jealous of her success which can be another trait of NPD.

Narcissists will often attract and marry submissive partners, who will be treated like a child and criticized in a way that the children in the family are. They will become enablers rescuing the mother. Her happiness will be paramount, because if mum is happy then everyone else's life will be pleasant. They will avoid confrontation and due to this will not defend the child for fear of the repercussions from the NPD. The child is then brought up in an unsupportive and unprotected environment.

"ME. ME, ME"
An inside look into the fragile heart of a self-absorbed mother

Mum is the puppeteer controlling every move within the household. Often in the relationship between the parents there will be times when both parents are not talking to each other (the silent treatment is the narcissists strongest weapon), the children will be used to pass communications between the two.

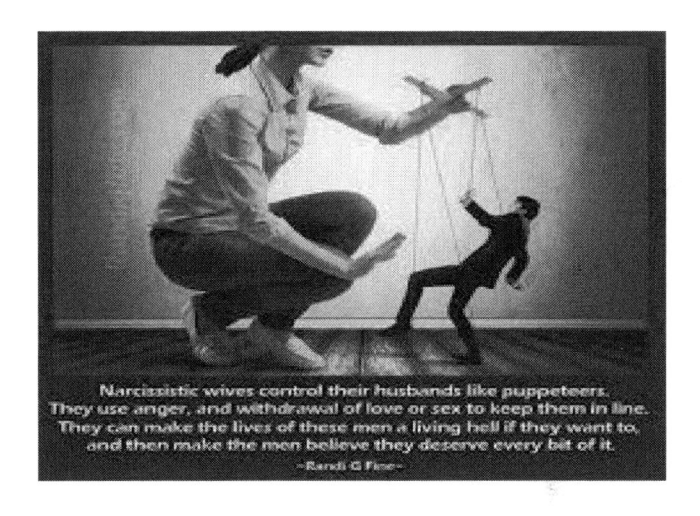

> Narcissistic wives control their husbands like puppeteers. They use anger, and withdrawal of love or sex to keep them in line. They can make the lives of these men a living hell if they want to, and then make the men believe they deserve every bit of it.
> ~Randi G Fine~

There comes a point when everyone in the family unit will pamper to meet the mother's needs. Everyone will tip toe around, walking on eggshells ensuring that mum is happy and taking responsibility for the NPD's feelings.

Having said all of this we all have narcissistic traits which are deemed healthy. Also be mindful that not all narcissists will display all of these behaviours and equally not all people who occasionally display some of these behaviours are narcissists.

We all have 'me, me, me' days and so we should. It is when the narcissism is on a daily or weekly basis that it can become

"ME. ME, ME"
An inside look into the fragile heart of a self-absorbed mother

unhealthy particularly for the child that needs so desperately to be loved, understood and empathised with.

"ME. ME, ME"
An inside look into the fragile heart of a self-absorbed mother

Chapter Two
Symptoms of a narcissistic mother

If you are reading this book because you believe that you are the child of a narcissistic parent, then you may find it difficult to connect the criteria in chapter one to your parent, so let me help you to make those connections in terms of parents that display narcissistic behaviours.

Be mindful that these symptoms will come in varying degrees. I also recognise through my work that there is the 'Covert Narcissist' and the 'Overt Narcissist' which means that some of them will display behaviours openly which will be clearer to recognise whereas others will display more closed behaviours which are not so easy to identify.

1. **An exaggerated sense of self importance**

    Is a person who talks about their self a lot. They minimise anyone else's contribution to the event. For example "I ran the office and dealt with everything and that office ran perfectly. I didn't get any help at all. I was the best manager they have ever had."

"ME. ME, ME"
An inside look into the fragile heart of a self-absorbed mother

They even have to be cleverer more beautiful and more successful than their offspring. A story that emphasises this is a dinner party where a boy meets his girlfriend's mother for the first time:

> **Mum:** Do you think I am more beautiful than my daughter?
>
> **Boy:** uhmm... (feeling uncomfortable and unsure how to answer this without offending the mother)
>
> **Mum:** She has her father's short height and squinty eyes where as I am taller giving me a more sophisticate look.

2. **Preoccupation with fantasies of unlimited success, power, brilliance, beauty or ideal love.**

   Is a person that tells you of all their achievements which you know not to be true. When you talk about a success of your own the NPD will outrank that success, whether that is academic success or winning a beauty pageant they will have done bigger and better.

3. **Believes they are special and can only be understood by, or associate with, other special or high status people.**

"ME. ME, ME"
An inside look into the fragile heart of a self-absorbed mother

They will see everyone who is normal as not special enough, not clever enough, not pretty enough.

4. **Requires excessive admiration**

   They like praise and compliments more than most and want to be told that everything they do is better than what others do. It is not important to them if the compliment givers are sincere or not they just need frequency. They may for example boast about how many birthday cards they have to emphasise how important and loved they are.

5. **Has a sense of entitlement**

   They expect compliance from everyone and expect special treatment. For example they may push to the front of queues believing that they have the right to go first. They believe that everyone should stop what they are doing to meet their demands.

6. **Selfishly takes advantage of others to achieve her own needs**

   They may be very manipulative and will have adapted strategies to get people to do what they want, with no care about how this may leave them feeling.

"ME. ME, ME"
An inside look into the fragile heart of a self-absorbed mother

7. **Lacks empathy**

   They will be able to talk about their feelings, but have no understanding of your feelings. They will tune out when you talk about your problems or dismiss yours and talk about themselves. They will have an inability to recognise and accurately interpret other people's emotions.

8. **Is often envious of others or believes others are envious of them**

   They will demonstrate behaviours linked to jealousy i.e. undermine what others including you have done. They will demonstrate behaviours that are linked to jealousy and if confronted by others justify their behaviour towards them to be that of envy.

9. **Shows arrogant, haughty, patronising or contemptuous behaviours or attitudes**

   They may treat other people badly, particularly if they have upset them. They will be very self righteous and expect loyalty but show no loyalty to others.

Be mindful that the NPD will not perhaps recognise these behaviours and some of their behaviours may be out of their

"ME. ME, ME"
An inside look into the fragile heart of a self-absorbed mother

conscious awareness. Those that they are aware of they will never admit to.

It is so important to a self absorbed mother that she is perfect in every way. To be faced with her imperfections can be very painful. She has an internal emotional wound which is overwhelmingly painful that she will protect with denial, vindictive behaviour and projection (which you will read more about further in this book).

"ME. ME, ME"
An inside look into the fragile heart of a self-absorbed mother

Chapter Three
What made your mother who she is and why can't she empathise?

There are many theories around which will tell you why a narcissist becomes a narcissist. These include Biological, Social, Environmental and Psychological Factors. It is also said that mismatches in parent-child relationships with either excessive pampering or excessive parenting is a feature of a child developing NPD.

I only feel knowledgeable enough to be able to explore the psychological factors although there does appear to be some evidence that it can be genetic due to the amount of NPD's within families, although equally this could also be learned behaviour. If you never receive or experience love then how can you then show love?

Another theory is that if a child internalises a lack of love in their own family and does not get their emotional needs met at some point in their developmental stage then they may end up developing narcissistic tendencies.

If as a child they have had to compete for attention within a large family for example and have not received that attention

"ME, ME, ME"
An inside look into the fragile heart of a self-absorbed mother

then they will develop all types of strategies to gain that attention, this behaviour then carries into adulthood.

Other hypotheses are that NPD links to the lack of emotional attachment that the child has had with their parent from birth. If the mother was an alcoholic or drug user or suffering with her own mental health or relationship difficulties such as being in a violent relationship then she would have been unable to meet the child's emotional needs adequately. Equally the cause of Narcissism can also be linked to children that have experienced physical, emotional and sexual abuse as children.

So as you can see there are no clear cut concepts for the development of people with narcissistic behaviours, so it can all seem very confusing. Perhaps there never will be. Perhaps it is about working with the effects rather than trying to find out the cause. Chances are we will never know the cause of a parent's NPD behaviours as the culture of narcissists is to be very secretive about the 'parts' of them that they deem unacceptable. That with the fact that not many will admit to having 'anything wrong with them' so do not access therapy or help, which is where the research begins may mean that a cause will be harder to determine.

Whatever the cause, the fact is that it is not your mums fault and they are unlikely to be fully consciously aware of their disorder or the impact that this disorder has on others including their children. They believe that the way that they view the world is the same as the way everyone else views the world.

One of the biggest signs of a narcissist is their inability to empathise. Empathy is the experience of understanding another

"ME. ME, ME"
An inside look into the fragile heart of a self-absorbed mother

person's feelings, thoughts and behaviours from their perspective. It is being able to step into another person's shoes and feel what they are feeling. Most of us can listen to a person's story and experience at some level how that person might be feeling whereas a narcissist can't.

They can only experience their own feelings. They are unable to step outside and tune in to what other people experience, especially those who feel, think and believe differently from them. They are unable to see things from another person's perspective; they can only see things from their own reality. They are locked inside their self centred world resulting in emotional isolation and a disconnection from others feelings and views.

Although the narcissist mum cannot empathise, she can however sympathise. There is a clear difference between sympathy and empathy.

Sympathy *is acknowledging another person's emotional experience. It is an ability to reflect understanding of another person's situation but viewed through their own lens.*

Empathy *is being able to experience what the other person is experiencing from their lens, seeing and feeling things from their perspective. It is the ability to step outside of yourself and enter the internal world of the other person.*

So a narcissist for example will be able to sympathise with a 'relationship breakdown' by relating it to their own experience

"ME. ME, ME"
An inside look into the fragile heart of a self-absorbed mother

of this particular problem. They will feel it as they felt it, but they will be unable to 'feel it' as you feel it. They do not have the ability to connect with other people's emotions only their own.

Somewhere along their developmental path they have not been able to connect with the feelings for others. They may have disassociated themselves from these feelings as it has become too painful for them. Maybe they witnessed abuse of significant others in their life, felt out of control and unable to stop the abuse but not the feelings associated with it so learned to switch off their empathy button and remain unaffected. Having switched off their empathy button it has remained in that off position. Or maybe they have such overwhelming feelings of their own that to feel what everyone else is feeling is just too much.

Another factor for the lack of empathy is if one or both parents did not encourage the expression of feelings while growing up, they may have disliked showing or other people showing intense emotion and maybe even denied its very existence. It is not surprising then if empathy is a mystery to them as they become adults.

It can never the less be very frustrating and hurtful when you have a mum that is unable to feel what you are feeling. Most mums feel the pain of their children's pain. When their children hurt they hurt. The self absorbed mum is unable to do this and they often rush into advice giving, trying desperately to offer a quick fix for the child so that it doesn't cause too much disruption to their own lives, when all the child wants is

"ME. ME, ME"
An inside look into the fragile heart of a self-absorbed mother

empathy. For the parent to stop what they are doing, truly listen and feel what it is like for them in their world.

"ME. ME, ME"
An inside look into the fragile heart of a self-absorbed mother

Chapter Four
When did you notice your mum was different?

As we are growing up it is natural for us to compare our friend's mums with our own, and equally as natural for us to feel that everyone else's mother is so much better than our own especially when we compare the boundaries of our own parents and the boundaries of our peer's parents. We all raise our children differently and the grass can always look greener on the other side.

However there are some traits typical of narcissistic mothers that are not necessarily the norm. I will endeavour to try and explain them as follows:

- They desperately crave unconditional love from their child although do not necessarily offer the same for them.

- They may try to create 'mini me's' living their life through the child encouraging them to do activities that they wanted to do, but for some reason or another never got the chance.

"ME. ME, ME"
An inside look into the fragile heart of a self-absorbed mother

- They don't like their child showing independence, they encourage dependency upon them.

- They may smother and protect their child under the guise that they are taking care of them

- They cannot handle normal childhood emotions and use phrases such as "you are over reacting" or "stop crying over spilt milk."

- They very rarely drive them to activities not chosen by them i.e. soccer practice, friend's houses or encourage friends to visit their house.

- They are not the first parent up the school if the child is being bullied or abused. They have no empathy and often just dismiss the child's cries for help when they are bulled by others.

- They will fail to provide age appropriate information on such things as menstruation, personal grooming, budgeting money and dating. This all serves to keep their children under their control.

- They will delegate household chores to the children as early as possible.

"ME. ME, ME"
An inside look into the fragile heart of a self-absorbed mother

- They will insist that they pay for their own personal items and clothing as early as possible.

- Older children may be expected to become responsible for younger children.

- They will expect perfectionism very early on in the child's life.

- They will expect their children to present as they are the ideal family and not discuss any imperfections within the family unit to others.

- They have a tendency to rewrite history in an attempt to hide any of their own imperfections.

- They will use terms such as "All I have done for you and you behave in this way" or "treat me like this."

- They will withhold their love if they perceive that you behaved badly.

- They will use you to communicate with others that they are in dispute with (i.e. husband, partners, friends, siblings etc) so you become the scapegoat as once relationships with these others are reconciled then you will remain the 'bad guy'

"ME. ME, ME"
An inside look into the fragile heart of a self-absorbed mother

- They expect and demand loyalty although very rarely give it.

- They will be very envious of you although will not admit to it.

- Siblings will either be the 'golden child' or the 'black sheep' and this can be changeable.

- They will dislike most if not all of your friends and partners as they will be seen to be taking your attention away from them.

- They will push you away when you need a hug or kiss although not when they need that hug or kiss.

- Their love and value will be dependent on what you can **'<u>do</u>'** for them.

- When you fall over and hurt yourself they will focus more on your dirty knees or clothes then on your wound and their interventions will be ones to stop you crying.

- They will push you to do well at school but this will not be for your benefit but for theirs to boast about to others to make them look good.

"ME. ME, ME"
An inside look into the fragile heart of a self-absorbed mother

- They will be hard to please and they are often very materialistic.

- Their punishments for your own negative behaviour may be slightly sadistic, humiliating or embarrassing.

- They may well tell lies to meet their own needs or to cover their own embarrassment about their own negative behaviour.

- They will discount and deny your memories and replace them with more favourable ones of their own.

- They have to be the centre of attention all of the time, they will steal the spotlight or spoil any occasion if someone else is the centre of attention.

- When confronted with something they have done, they may well tell you that you have a 'very vivid imagination' or that they have 'no idea what you are talking about.'

- They can be very self absorbed. Their feelings, needs and wants are very important and yours are irrelevant or insignificant.

- If you have gone through a painful experience, they may focus on how that experience has affected them.

"ME, ME, ME"
An inside look into the fragile heart of a self-absorbed mother

- They can be very defensive and extremely sensitive to criticism.

- They can be childish and petty and can be seen to 'get even' with significant others that have hurt them.

- They rarely ask, they demand.

- They will be good organisers, however will throw in the towel if anyone dares to give constructive feedback or criticize their attempts.

- They are unable to take 'no' for an answer and will push, arm twist or manipulate until they get their own way.

- They are never wrong about anything. They will never, ever genuinely apologise for anything that they have done or said.

- They will struggle to understand your need for privacy and may invade this privacy to gain control.

- They ask people (inc you) how they are but doesn't listen to the reply, they just want to get other peoples stuff out the way so that they can then focus on their own stuff.

- They can be phoney or overdramatic

"ME. ME, ME"
An inside look into the fragile heart of a self-absorbed mother

- They can also be incongruently very charming

- If you've got a cold then they will have the flu.

- One of their forms of punishment will be the 'silent treatment' if you disagree, confront them or don't meet their needs.

- Another form of punishment will be that they speak to you in curt clipped sentences or will be histrionic to shut down any rational conversation.

- They may tell other people how wonderful you are to impress or to get them to do more, but never tell you.

- Their husband/partners will never have time for you because s/he is trying to meet all the needs of your mum. To stay in the relationship and maintain peace in their own lives they have to do this. In some cases they may almost worship her.

- Bargaining "if you do this for me, then I will do this for you"

- Children of narcissistic parents must do as they are told or risk shame, guilt, anger or even in some cases physical abuse.

"ME. ME, ME"
An inside look into the fragile heart of a self-absorbed mother

- Their children may sometimes be put in situations of danger if the narcissist wants them out of the way for them to 'do their own thing.'

- Ignores or overwhelms the child.

- Places their own emotions on to the child if they are upset by someone else.

- Sometimes neglects the child's needs putting their own first.

- Treats others as objects and not people.

- They will think nothing of eating food off someone else's plate.

- They have a short memory when it comes to anything that they have done that is negative, however a long memory when it comes to remembering anything they perceive you have done which is deemed negative.

- Your accomplishments are acknowledged only to the extent that they can take the credit for themselves. Any success or accomplishments for which they cannot take credit is ignored or diminished.

"ME, ME, ME"
An inside look into the fragile heart of a self-absorbed mother

- If there is an occasion whereby you are to be the centre of attention and there is no opportunity for them to be the centre of attention, they will try to prevent the occasion, threaten to not come, not attend or come and leave early.

- Creates a division between siblings or other family members.

- After years of 'doing' for them, they will say that you have done 'nothing!'

- They will snub or discard people without a blink if they feel scorned by them.

- They will drop 'a bombshell' prior to any occasion whereby you are to achieve success or be centre stage.

- They will minimise any of your achievements if they outrank hers.

- They may call you 'selfish' if you try to express or get your own needs met.

- When something upsets you they will say things such as 'don't make a fuss.'

- They will play the victim often and tell people that they have done their best for you and that you have hurt them

"ME, ME, ME"
An inside look into the fragile heart of a self-absorbed mother

very much. That they would do anything to make you happy, but they don't know what to do as you keep pushing them away when all they want to do is help you.

- They are always working on ways to get what other people have including their children. If their child gets a new washing machine they will want one too.

- They are envious of the child's relationships, whether they are friendships or love relationships.

- A common phrase of a NPD mother is "Don't wash your or our dirty linen in public." They would be horrified for outsiders to see any 'badness' in their family.

- If they feel wounded then they can be very vindictive in their attempt to wound back.

- They will always need to have the last word.

- They are unable to keep confidences, and will share confidences to achieve a high status among the family, making each child feel 'the special one' to be privy to these confidences.

- You're responsible for their feelings; however they have no responsibility for yours.

"ME, ME, ME"
An inside look into the fragile heart of a self-absorbed mother

- They claim to be unable to remember bad things they have done and if you try to jog their memory they will respond with "Why do you have to bring up the past" or why do you have to dredge up your old grudges?"

- NPD mothers love to be waited on and often intersperse their children with little requests such as "while you are up...."

- They may wear you down with histrionics, pouting and the silent treatment so you're more inclined to do what they want.

- Any chores that they need you to do are needed to be done now this minute, or at her convenience and not yours. The chore will be urgent unless the time you can do it interferes with something that they are doing.

- If they visit you or you visit them, you are required to spend all your time with them. Lord help you if you give your attention to your husband or your children, they will pout, sulk, manipulate or give you the silent treatment. Entertaining themselves is unthinkable.

- If you are communicating with other people then they have a tendency to 'but in' and inevitably bring the conversation around to them.

"ME. ME, ME"
An inside look into the fragile heart of a self-absorbed mother

- They cannot cope with silent time. If you are engrossed in a book or tv programme, they will constantly interrupt you.

- They enjoy seeing yours and others pain and will think up ways to instil this in a way they won't be seen as bad and can cover themselves by saying it was a joke. The pain of others entertains them.

- As you get older they will directly or indirectly place responsibility for their welfare and their emotions on to you, weeping on your shoulder and unloading on you any time something goes awry for them.

- If you tell them that they cannot do something they will do it anyway so that you either have to give in or be the 'bad guy' so that they can then show people how bad you are and show you that you can't say 'no' to them.

- They will expect others to carry their bags, they do not ask they will just dump them in your path and walk off.

- If you give a NPD a Christmas gift that they do not like, you can bet your bottom dollar that either you or someone else will get it back the following year.

- Their problems demand your full and immediate attention, yours are brushed aside.

"ME, ME, ME"
An inside look into the fragile heart of a self-absorbed mother

- They are never wrong about anything.

- You were never allowed to be needy or have bad feelings or problems. Those experiences were only for her, and you were responsible for making it right for her.

These are a few of the things you may have noticed growing up and as an adult in a relationship with your mother.

You may even have believed them to be the norm and most definitely accepted them as part of your mum's personality, which they were. But they are the traits of a self absorbed personality and will most definitely have had an effect on you both as a child and as an adult in your own significant relationships.

Be mindful though that there is a degree of narcissism in most of us as parents. We take pride in our children's achievements and feel that their achievements reflect well upon us. Likewise when our children do something that we are proud of we proudly tell our friends of their achievements. However the healthy parent while taking a kind of narcissistic pleasure in their achievements will see their child has having identities of their own.

"ME. ME, ME"
An inside look into the fragile heart of a self-absorbed mother

Chapter Five
Unhealthy behaviours that you may develop & how it affects your relationships

Unfortunately and although it would crucify the perfectionist mother to hear this, these mothers steal their child's childhood, identities and future healthy relationships.

Narcissists are incapable of loving anyone in any depth. It is incredibly difficult and painful to acknowledge that your mother never loved you without blaming yourself, without seeing yourself as unlovable and without the impact that this has on your own self esteem. How can you, when your mum raised you to blame yourself, you were her scapegoat.

I am hoping this book and the knowledge that I am sharing with you will help you to put the blame where it rightfully belongs – in the past and possibly far further in the past then your mother and even your grandmother belongs. This is not the parent's total fault, they have been raised like this, it may or may not be genetics or learned behaviour or it may be due to a dysfunction or untreated trauma in their psychopathology. Equally they may not know they are like they are, nor will they want to hear what they are like.

"ME. ME, ME"
An inside look into the fragile heart of a self-absorbed mother

I hope that when people read this book that this sinister disorder isn't perpetuated down the generations. It is not unusual for children of narcissists to become or have some narcissistic tendencies themselves. After all we learn how to behave from our caretakers.

Some clients when they enter the therapy room and have built up a trusting relationship with the therapist will release overwhelming emotions that they have stored up over years of suppressing feelings, believing that they are unacceptable, dramatic or too unmanageable for others.

They may display some narcissistic traits themselves, particularly their inability to empathise because to empathise brings them too close to and too in touch with their own painful emotions. They may have demonstrated some levels of narcissism to protect themselves from an overload of feelings as a method of self care and survival or equally they may have learned this behaviour from their own caretakers. However often these people are not narcissists and have a huge capacity to empathise with many issues once they have worked through their own pain.

It is important to recognise that during the child's upbringing there will have been other people in their life that had an influential effect on their life and depending on how healthy that relationship was will be dependent on how they become as an adult. For example if they had a grandparent that they spent a lot of time with or maybe even another parent that offered them unconditional love then the impact their mothers

"ME, ME, ME"
An inside look into the fragile heart of a self-absorbed mother

behaviour had on them will be minimised/counteracted by this other significant person

The behaviours, thoughts and feelings of children of narcissist mothers may be as follows:

- **People pleasing** – this is what they have always had to do growing up. They have always had to please their mothers to be loved. If they do not then their mother will withdraw that love. So long as their children are behaving properly a narcissist parent will be loving. That love disappears the moment a child doesn't meet the mother's expectations. The child of a narcissist will continue this behaviour into their adult relationships, both friendships and love relationships.

- **Suppression of feelings** – the child has learned from a young age that most of her negative feelings and some of her positive feelings are not acceptable. The children of a narcissist parent learn that their feelings are invalid; they will have learned to stifle their feelings to keep the peace. S/he has learned to cover these feelings with unauthentic feelings that were more acceptable in her world which can be confusing for the person she is with, in her adult relationships.

- **Tries to hard** – they try to 'do' everything in the relationship sometimes rescuing others because growing up s/he has been valued for what s/he **does** rather than for who s/he is.

"ME. ME, ME"
An inside look into the fragile heart of a self-absorbed mother

Also a lot of their life they have been validated for rescuing their mothers.

- o **Not good enough** – they often have a sense of not being 'good enough' this is often due to their mothers need for perfection from their children and sometimes harsh criticism for the smallest of crimes. Also maybe down to the alienation from the mother or indeed the family.

- o **Distorted view of love** – they may have a distorted view of love as they have learned that love is about "what I can do for you and what you can do for me."

- o **Unhealthy management of anger** – as anger is most definitely one of the emotions that would not be accepted in the narcissists' family they will have learned to suppress this emotion and may have the occasional outburst.

- o **Unmet needs** – when you have gone throughout your childhood having your needs unmet, discounted and ignored, it becomes increasingly difficult to ask for those needs to be met in adulthood. We begin to believe that we are undeserving of needs and wants or that our needs and wants are unrealistic.

- o **Perfectionism** – they have spent most of their life trying to be the perfect child and fear the withdrawal of love if they are not perfect. This resurrects feelings of guilt and shame

"ME, ME, ME"
An inside look into the fragile heart of a self-absorbed mother

that they continue this perfectionist behaviour in their adult relationships.

- **Lack of assertiveness** – they will have been discouraged from showing assertiveness and sometimes even punished for it so will not have learned these skills to great effect or be too scared of rejection to use these skills.

- **Dependency** – the mother will have set up situations where even as an adult the child is still dependent on their mother's validation. They will still go to their mother for praise, love and approval as adults and still be mortified if they don't receive this.

- **Patterns of abusive relationships** – the child of a narcissist parent will often be attracted to abusive/ narcissistic people as adults and find themselves in abusive relationships.

- **A sense of not belonging/fitting in** – this will have been put there or it may have been internalised by them from the messages of a narcissistic parent. They often feel the outsider within the family unit and also within friendship groups.

- **Need validation for decisions** – the narcissistic parent has taken away the child's thrive for independency as a form of control, leaving them now uncomfortable with their own decision making. Needing approval for their decisions.

"ME. ME, ME"
An inside look into the fragile heart of a self-absorbed mother

- **Responsibility** - they will take responsibility for everyone's behaviour and feelings as they have learned to take this responsibility as a child. To be responsible for their mothers happiness or equally sadness.

- **Rescuing** – they will rescue people which will usually result in it backfiring on them. This behaviour is due to them rescuing situations in their childhood to prevent mum becoming upset or angry.

- **Untrue to self** – they become adept at being who they think everyone else wants them to be rather than their true self. They develop a phoney self to gain acceptance from others. This is because they have learned to be who their mother wants them to be. They then struggle to be their authentic true self and many have been someone else for so long that they are unable to figure out who their authentic self is.

- **Suffer in silence** – the child will have been told from a very young age not to make a fuss, to suffer in silence, so as an adult they will continue to do this. They may be frightened to say how they feel or what they want for fear of causing trouble.

- **Powerless** – they often feel like a little girl and are often scared of their own power. They have difficulty setting boundaries with family members and others.

"ME, ME, ME"
An inside look into the fragile heart of a self-absorbed mother

- **Lack of self praise** – they will struggle to celebrate their successes, waiting for the put down or sting in the tail.

- **Inability to have fun** – many children of NPD parents fear having fun and this is due to the looks of disapproval when they have in their past. They can be seen as too serious. Equally they can let rip when out of sight of disapproving onlookers and be the life and soul of the party or pretend to be to gain the approval and acceptance of others.

- **Attention seeking** – they may have attention seeking behaviours of their own, as they have learned that this is the way to be loved or to make up for the lack of attention that they received as a child.

- **Ultra-sensitive to the moods of others** – Due to years of monitoring the mood of their mother's, children of NPD's develop an intuition of how others are feeling. This may leave them running around trying to 'fix' the mood of others in the same way as they did as children for their mother.

- **Minimising unacceptable behaviour** – they can make excuses for or be accepting of bad behaviour towards themselves and others to try to be more accepting than their mothers, or due to their own fear of rejection or abandonment if they do not accept the behaviour.

- **Tough Cookie -** A suppression of their own vulnerabilities.

"ME, ME, ME"
An inside look into the fragile heart of a self-absorbed mother

- o **Lack of trust** – When they have been unable to trust their mother it makes it difficult to be able to trust other people. They are always on guard waiting to be knocked off the throne.

For clients:

These are some of the behaviours that you may be aware that you do. You have picked this book up for a reason; you are reading it because it is raising some resonance. If after reading it you identify that your mother had some of these traits then you may also be able to identify some of your behaviours and the links that they have to your past. You may also have reached a point where you have recognised that these behaviours are not protecting you from pain anymore nor are they getting your own needs met. A therapist or/and self help material can help you to change your behaviours into more healthy ones.

You may have experienced several unsuccessful relationships. This may be because you are attracting partners that have narcissistic traits due to the way that you present to the outside world. Givers attract takers and the child of a narcissist is definitely very giving, to the point where it impacts on their own emotional and physical health.

It may be that your relationships fail due to both of your different interpretations of love. The child of an NPD has a very distorted view of love due to being raised with distorted love.

You may be experiencing intense pain about the way other people treat you, such as the 'silent treatment' and recognise that

"ME. ME, ME"
An inside look into the fragile heart of a self-absorbed mother

other people do not seem to experience the depth of pain that you experience. You may be struggling to understand why or how this behaviour is hooking into an old wound left by your NPD parent. Silence for you means a withdrawal of love, a rejection and can resurrect strong feelings of shame, guilt and not feeling good enough.

Whatever your reason don't be too hard on yourself these behaviours have developed from a young age as a coping strategy, a way of surviving the covert or overt abuse of a narcissistic mother. Well done for getting this far.

For therapists:

These are some of (not all) the behaviours that a child of a narcissist mother may present with. These behaviours will be creating many problems in their interpersonal relationships.

They may have had several unsuccessful relationships both platonic and sex relationships and have a lack of understanding of why this is. They can often present highly emotive or with a disassociation from their emotions, speaking about their feelings from an intellectual level and unable to connect with the raw emotion.

There may be transference in the relationship if they experience real or imagined discounting of their feelings. They may relate to you in the same way as they did their mothers, people please, be careful about what they say, say the things that they think you want them to say rather than what they are really thinking or feeling. They may suppress feelings such as anger or

"ME. ME, ME"
An inside look into the fragile heart of a self-absorbed mother

frustration with you the therapist. They may be sensitive to criticism or/and lack trust in you to accept them truly for who they are, therefore present in a phoney way. They will most definitely struggle with deep rooted emotions and if you get close to those emotions they will use avoidance strategies to protect themselves. They often speak from a cognitive level rather than from an emotive level. They will keep their distance waiting for a time when you will reject them. Equally there is the risk of a dependency when you do validate their feelings which they may experience as the 'ideal mother.'

"ME. ME, ME"
An inside look into the fragile heart of a self-absorbed mother

Chapter Six
All you do for her and still feel unloved, praise with a sting in the tail & I can do better than that

It is hard for survivors to deal with the fact that after all they have said and done for their self absorbed mother and all the hoops that they have jumped through, all the sacrifices they have made and still they can't get this person to love or understand them or give them the relationship that they so desperately want.

Still they say that you are bad or have never done anything for them. Still they will call you the selfish one. This can be immensely frustrating but a typical indicator of anyone that has been in a narcissistic relationship. The more they are pushed away, abused, or abandoned the harder they will try to get the narcissists love. A love they have an inability to give. It will be like getting a stocking off a bare leg, it is virtually impossible to gain love and understanding from a narcissist.

Clients often come into therapy with the belief that there is something wrong with them. It is extremely hard for them to accept that there are mothers out there who are incapable of

"ME. ME, ME"
An inside look into the fragile heart of a self-absorbed mother

loving them in the way they need to be loved and even harder to accept that their mother may be one of them.

Children of narcissistic mothers find it difficult to receive praise or any form of positive feedback because in their past when they have received praise there has always been a sting in the tail. For example "you did very well in your dance show but you need to smile more everyone else was smiling and you looked miserable." "You have 5 out of 6 A's in your school report, but what about this one D you really do need to try harder!" A favourite is "I'm telling you this because I love you........." followed by some crushing slaughter of your character. It is no wonder that children of NPD's develop a low self esteem of their own and they never, ever feel quite 'good enough.'

Bear in mind that the NPD mother will always say that they have got your best interests at heart and they truly do believe that they have. It is extremely hard for them to give you praise without the sting in the tail because they have such a low self esteem themselves.

People with low self esteem in general find it difficult to give praise. Equally the NPD finds it uncomfortable if someone else praises you too. They will do one of three things say "yes but she lets herself down in this way ...." and finds something else that you are not so good at or say "yes but what about me I am good at that too" or "she gets that from me."

This of course, draws the attention back to her. It's not too bad in the scheme of things but quite irritating to say the least.

"ME. ME, ME"
An inside look into the fragile heart of a self-absorbed mother

Another irritating trait of the NPD mother is that whatever you have achieved in your life she will have done this, and you can bet your bottom dollar that she will have done it better.

Conversations will run along the lines of:

Child: Mum, I have got a promotion at work (waiting for a congratulations or some sort of validation).

Mum: I got a promotion when I worked for the hospital I was put in charge of 12 people and they loved me as their manager they said I was the most supportive manager ever..........

OR

Child: Mum, I have passed my driving test.

Mum: When I passed my driving test **first time** I was so nervous but the examiner said that I did really well and that he had never seen a woman driver so confident..........

Equally when a child of a NPD discusses something with an NPD mum that may threaten the dependency s/he has on their mother she will respond with something negative, putting some spanner in the works to burst the child's bubble and try to sabotage the child's attempt at independence i.e.

"ME. ME, ME"
An inside look into the fragile heart of a self-absorbed mother

> **Child:** Mum I have met this amazing man he is from Scotland and I think that I have fallen in love.
> **Mum:** Oh you be careful, he will no doubt be an alcoholic and they are known for beating up women.

OR

> **Child:** I have been give a great job opportunity but it is in London a hundred miles away but it is too good to turn down.
> **Mum:** How are you going to cope on your own there and accommodation is so expensive.

They can be very negative about any acts of dependency that the child may have and they find it difficult to understand why there mother is so negative when everyone else in their life is pleased for them.

NPD's find it very difficult when their offspring do something that facilitates change in the child's behaviour towards them. They are known to hate it when their child grows up and begins to develop independence and this is often a time of battles between mother and child, the child fighting for their independence and the mother fighting to keep control and the child dependent on them, even when they become adults. Their dependency on them to fulfil their needs is very strong.

"ME. ME, ME"
An inside look into the fragile heart of a self-absorbed mother

As adult children the battle does not cease. A new relationship that empowers the child to be more assertive can be threatening to the narcissist mum.

If the child does a psychology course or accesses personal therapy and begins to make changes in his/her relationship with their mother it will create disturbances in the mothers psyche. They will make comments such as:

> "You have changed since you started that psychology course into a horrible person I miss my old daughter/son who was so loving and caring"

What they really mean is they want the adoring, people pleasing, dependent and compliant child back. The NPD parent will do anything to get that child back and if the child stands by their guns and refuses to budge then they will likely to be punished and alienated from the family – back to the black sheep or scapegoat, no longer the golden child. (See next chapter)

This can be very painful for the developing child because there they are doing something to better their life, to enable them to function more healthily and still they are being punished. They have not committed some heinous crime, they have not got pregnant out of wedlock and they have not ended up as a drop out our taken illicit drugs and yet still they are being punished. It can be extremely confusing and leave the child with the feeling that they cannot do right for wrong.

"ME. ME, ME"
An inside look into the fragile heart of a self-absorbed mother

It can be very soul destroying when you run to this self absorbed parent with some exciting news still trying to please, still hoping for validation and you get slammed down to the floor. Self esteem crushed again!

The important thing is that you are an adult now, independent and have to make and stand by your own decisions and validate your own actions. This is your mothers issue not yours!

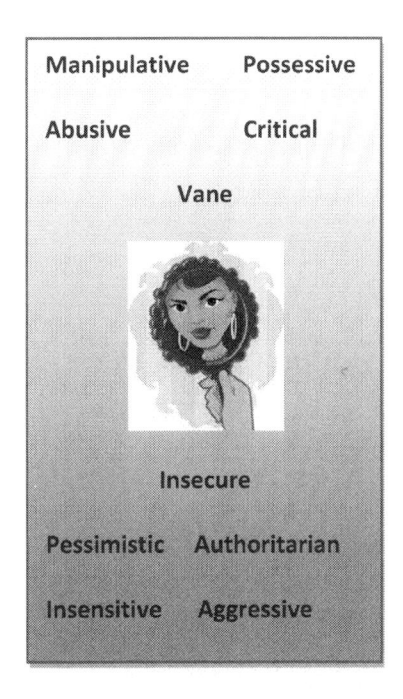

Manipulative	Possessive
Abusive	Critical

Vane

Insecure

Pessimistic	Authoritarian
Insensitive	Aggressive

"ME. ME, ME"
An inside look into the fragile heart of a self-absorbed mother

Chapter Seven
Scapegoating versus the golden child versus the black sheep

If there are several children in a narcissistic household then you may have recognised the dynamics of the family in terms of the 'golden child' versus 'the black sheep' and also there may be 'the scapegoat' within the family. This can cause major friction between the siblings and quite rightfully jealousy.

Golden child – is the child that can never do wrong, s/he is the child that achieves all the best grades, (even the most minor achievements are praised and celebrated). S/he is the best behaved, the child that always says 'yes', they do all the household chores and nothing is too much for them. They are 'mummy's little star, little helper and little angel.' Mum will go to great lengths to tell the rest of you how wonderful s/he is and how rotten the rest of you are.

Black Sheep – this is the child that has started to develop his/her independence, the one that has separated them self from the parent, the one that will confront the parents behaviour and

"ME. ME, ME"
An inside look into the fragile heart of a self-absorbed mother

the one who dares to say "No" I am unable to do that right now" because s/he has their own life. As the golden boy can do no wrong the black sheep can do no right. S/he is punished for the most minor offences. The punishment can be anything from disapproving looks, short clipped tones when talking to her, silent treatment to vindictiveness.

The Scapegoat – this is usually the weakest of the litter the one that is eager to please but falls below mums levels of perfection, in animal terms this child would be called the 'runt of the litter.' This is the child that is easily stage-managed and is usually manipulated into doing all the things that the NPD feels uncomfortable doing including confronting others that have hurt the NPD. They will be the ones that the NPD will blame for carrying out the actions of the NPD. The self absorbed mother will get the scapegoat to do something for her, and if the NPD is confronted about it then she will tell others that it wasn't her idea it was the 'scapegoats'. The scapegoat is to blame for all the family woes.

Be mindful that anyone of the children can fall off their 'golden child' pedestal at any time and become one of the more negative positions, although sometimes one or more children can seem to have the more permanent position of the golden child. Equally one person can be both the scapegoat and the black sheep, or the golden child and the unaware scapegoat.

So, for example if someone upsets the NPD she will play the hurt victim. The golden child may jump into defending the NPD

"ME. ME, ME"
An inside look into the fragile heart of a self-absorbed mother

or may even be asked to. S/he may do this to maintain the position of golden child. By the same token the Black sheep may be manipulated into protecting the NPD to raise their position to golden child.

Either way if the NPD is confronted by the person who upset them, they will deny all knowledge of their child's involvement and attribute the blame on to the child.

There is sometimes a shift between positions within the family particularly if it benefits the NPD or if she needs to punish one of her children or needs more attention. This is often why the children try so hard to please their parent to gain the 'golden child' status and feel loved.

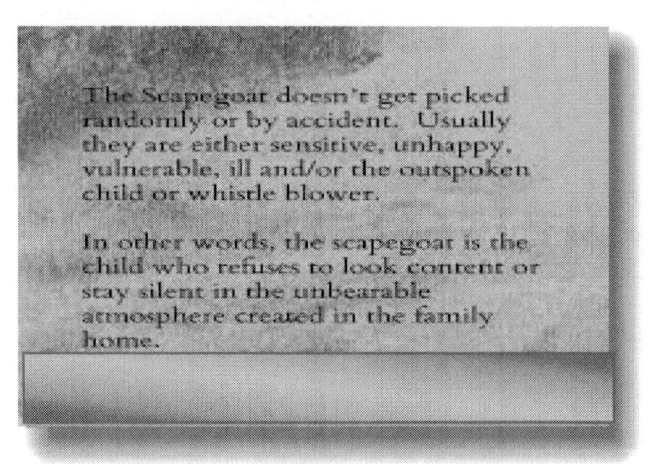

> The Scapegoat doesn't get picked randomly or by accident. Usually they are either sensitive, unhappy, vulnerable, ill and/or the outspoken child or whistle blower.
>
> In other words, the scapegoat is the child who refuses to look content or stay silent in the unbearable atmosphere created in the family home.

Understandably the scapegoat/black sheep sees the mother in a negative way and will try to explain their experiences of the mother to the golden child. However as like most people that find themselves privileged, the golden child does not see the mother's unfairness and they tend to excuse her behaviour.

"ME. ME, ME"
An inside look into the fragile heart of a self-absorbed mother

In some instances the golden child may be recruited by the narcissist to behave in the same way as she does towards the black sheep or/and scapegoat.

Narcissist mothers give the overt or covert message that her children cannot and must not discuss her in a negative way with each other. Therefore the mother's behaviour never gets talked about so discrepancies in stories, family dynamics or experiences never get resolved.

In the NPD family often children don't communicate except through their mother. She frequently creates conflict between the siblings and as they have learned that 'silence' is how one handles conflict then they will have no communication with each other at all. This then gives her control, she can decide what everyone hears and it is always her interpretations.

The narcissist mother also uses favouritism and gossip to control her children's relationships and to maintain the divide and rule she has created. In their adult lives she will keep each of her children informed of what the others are doing passing on lots of 'juicy gossip' which is always disguised as concern, but in a way that will raise contempt rather than compassion.

The NPD will never praise you to your face but will praise you to your siblings, particularly to the one who is not doing well. You can do fifty jobs for her but she will tell you all about the one job that your sibling did and how good s/he is. This ultimately creates envy within the family. This envy however will be towards the sibling and not the NPD parent and will without a doubt cause resentments and separation. The children will become angry with each other although will not show it in

"ME. ME, ME"
An inside look into the fragile heart of a self-absorbed mother

view of the fact that anger is an unpermitted emotion. Consequently leaving feelings hovering in the air, 'an elephant that is always in the room' at family gatherings.

The end result of the NPD parents' behaviour is a family in which almost all, if not all communication is triangular. She stores all the information she can from each family member and although appears to have a very short memory re her own shortcomings she has an amazing memory re her children's. She then passes this on to the other siblings creating the resentments that prevent them from communicating freely with each other.

The NPD then has the only communication between the children which is exactly the way she wants it! Does this end when the NPD parent dies? Don't hold your breath as her work may continue through the golden child if s/he has developed some or most of her narcissistic traits.

"ME. ME, ME"
An inside look into the fragile heart of a self-absorbed mother

Chapter Eight
Triangulation, Narcissistic Supply and Gaslighting

Narcissistic Supply is a term used to describe the oxygen that NPD's need or feed on to survive. The oxygen predominantly consists of attention, approval, admiration, esteem, love and adoration and in some cases fear. To leave someone feeling fearful can raise the NPD's self esteem and subsequently feed their supply.

We all have a need for approval, love affirmation, attention and sometimes adoration. However the difference between normal narcissistic supply and that of an NPD is that we can survive without it, we would feel uncomfortable if we were oozing with it.

The narcissist has to be oozing in it they are in a sense addicted to it and most of their behaviours will be to attract it. They need it to regulate their low self worth. Without a narcissistic supply they will crumble and become dysfunctional. They have developed over many years a 'false self' – they pretend to be something they are not to gain it.

Narcissists have a very low or no self esteem and they will blow your candle out to make theirs shine brighter. Their

"ME. ME, ME"
An inside look into the fragile heart of a self-absorbed mother

manipulation and strategic tactics are all about gaining self esteem, (oxygen) that will make them feel better about themselves.

This is often why they will humiliate and embarrass people in public. They will play all sorts of games to get attention, approval and adoration to feed their supply.

Triangulation is a schema used by the narcissistic parent to change the balance of power within the family. The NPD parent's mentality is the 'divide and rule' mentality. They will be at their happiest when their siblings are not friends with each other, after some conflict that the NPD will have manipulatively instigated in one shape or form. Whereas most parents would be upset that their children are at loggerheads with each other and try to encourage a resolution between the siblings, the NPD will thrive on this. This to gain control of the way information flows, the way it is interpreted adding their own tinge to the story. This is also used as a way for them to feed narcissistic supply.

It is not unusual in families of a narcissist for siblings or relations to be estranged or in conflict with each other. Often because they don't talk to each other they are not aware that the puppeteer, the NPD is playing one off against the other. The reason this is maintained is from the long term messages that no-one in the household is allowed to talk about the NPD in a negative way.

The messages that the NPD gives their children over the years are either overt or covert such as the disapproving looks,

"ME. ME, ME"
An inside look into the fragile heart of a self-absorbed mother

the silent treatments, threats and withdrawals of love and sometimes threats of suicide if they do or say anything that risks their self esteem.

The siblings often compete with each other to become the 'golden child.' No one wants to be the 'blacksheep' or the 'scapegoat' that the NPD blames everything on. So the dynamics inevitably causes tension between the siblings.

If the siblings did find the strength to get together and communicate about the behaviours of the NPD they would without a doubt find that the NPD had called one child to another telling a variation of inconsistent stories.

However the fear of the NPD finding out, (who will have created a lack of trust within the family), and being alienated, alongside the possible unconscious fear of hearing that their parent was telling lies about them that reinforces an underlying belief that they are not loved would be too painful. So, the secret remains, nothing is confronted and the NPD continues to manipulate and control her family in a way that feeds her supply.

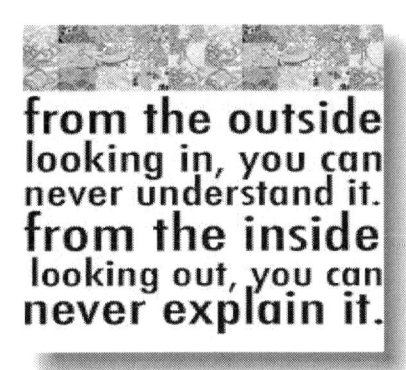

from the outside looking in, you can never understand it. from the inside looking out, you can never explain it.

"ME. ME, ME"
An inside look into the fragile heart of a self-absorbed mother

Gaslighting is a way in which NPD parents lie for their own gain – intentional or not we will probably never know – but it can often leave the child question their own sanity. The NPD will change history, put their own slant on the story and rewrite an incident all to protect themselves from being or feeling bad. Narcissists gaslight routinely and if you challenge these 'lies' then you will be told directly or indirectly that you have an overactive imagination, that you are mad, unreasonable or a drama queen. She may even diagnose you as being neurotic or psychotic and will only talk to you when you have calmed down or come to your senses. When they gaslight they are telling you that your memory and perceptions are mistaken, it's effectively saying that you are crazy.

Gaslighting can be one of the most frustrating things about NPD's and they can be so convincing and so inflexible with their belief that the child or significant other (because they do it with everyone) can feel like s/he is going crazy. Gaslighting can be one of the most insidious forms of emotional and psychological abuse.

What you may see the NPD doing frequently too is take the credit in a story and paint themselves as the hero when it was you or someone else all along.

"ME, ME, ME"
An inside look into the fragile heart of a self-absorbed mother

Chapter Nine
Projection, silent treatment, hoovering & the flying monkeys

Projection is a theory which was conceptualised by **Sigmund Freud.** He considered that we project our thoughts, motivations, desires and feelings that we cannot accept about ourselves on to others.

In psychology it is described as a defence mechanism that involves taking our own unacceptable qualities or feelings and ascribing them to other people.

For example someone who is opinionated but does not like this part of themselves may frequently call other people opinionated. By attributing this on to others it prevents the person from feeling bad about them self.

This is a very typical behaviour of a narcissist and NPD mothers are not exempt from this. I have a client who is constantly told by her mother each time she expresses her feelings that she is a "me, me, me" person. This is ironic really when NPD's are known to be 'me, me, me.' This person does not like to internalise or feel the selfishness that she experiences and portrays, and so projects this on to others.

"ME. ME, ME"
An inside look into the fragile heart of a self-absorbed mother

Projection is a way of distancing ourselves from our own dysfunction. NPD's are threatened by people that are selfless, honest, caring, empathic or loved. They will project their own selfish feelings on to the most selfless person, their lies on to the most honest and take pleasure in telling someone who is truly loved that their partner does not love them.

They will tell other family members that their children do not want to see them when it is the NPD that does not want to see the child. She is punishing them for confronting the part of herself that she does not want to look at.

In some instances NPD's will stop Grandparents or other relatives from seeing their children to control their children or to punish the relatives for confronting their behaviour, or for not jumping to their unrealistic demands.

The most painful thing about having a NPD parent or indeed family member is that they will make all sorts of accusations and call you heinous names, which you will know at an intellectual level are not true but on an emotional level will tear you apart.

One of a narcissist favourite projections are "It is always about you!!!" It is quite frustrating when they accuse you of all the things that they are, do and say.

The important thing to remember is that when a narcissist accuses you s/he is actually speaking to a mirror. The narcissist's accusations about your character are exactly what the narcissist feels internally about him/herself.

The narcissist will use any trick or method available to project their thoughts, feelings and behaviours on to you, such as

"ME, ME, ME"
An inside look into the fragile heart of a self-absorbed mother

lying, distorting and exaggerating. They will use third parties as evidence which will most probably be fabricated or the third party will just have agreed to avoid the aftermath of disagreeing.

They will even lie about situations whereby you were present and witnessed the truth, sticking to their version of events through thick and thin. The annoying thing we have to learn about these personalities is that they actually believe their version of the truth. These behaviours leave their 'victims' struggling to prove him/herself, feeling angry and frustrated and sometimes as if they are going insane. They can leave you confused, shocked, heartbroken and depleted of energy.

As a child when a narcissistic parent behaved in this way they were defenceless, they lacked understanding and insight. They had no words to describe what the parent was doing or how this left them feeling. The child would feel at fault, s/he would feel a great sense of shame and try harder to make his/her parent love them. Subsequently the child would develop strategies of their own to survive. These would then become their learned behaviours that they would then carry into their future relationships. (See chapter 5).

NARCISSISTS PRAISE SOFTLY, BLAME LOUDLY

Narcissists project their own disturbing psychopathy onto others, accusing others of the very same behavior that they are guilty of

© BreakingUpWithYourNarcissist.com

"ME. ME, ME"
An inside look into the fragile heart of a self-absorbed mother

Silent treatment is a form of bullying it is a form of abuse which is often used to control, punish, and test boundaries or to avoid issues and responsibilities. Narcissistic mothers are renowned for using this as a form of control if they are unhappy or angry with their child, and whereas most adults would just take this behaviour with a pinch of salt, for the child of a narcissist parent it can be very painful.

Although the narcissist's frequent use of the silent treatment may seem like a relief from their criticism and rages, it can be just as damaging to the victim as other forms of emotional and psychological abuse. To them it can feel like the ultimate rejection, it clearly states to them that they are not loved, accepted and are not good enough to be part of this family. They are not good enough or worthy enough to have their mothers love. This fear of the silent treatment is carried into their adult lives. This can create irrational thoughts and painful feelings when they perceive others as giving them the silent treatment, to the point where a friend ignoring them on the street can send them into sheer panic and hysteria, when realistically the friend may have just been in a world of their own.

When a narcissist mother uses the silent treatment they take it to the extreme. They will refuse or abstain from talking to someone for months and sometimes years. The person may cease to exist for an extensive and disproportionate length of time. They will be patiently waiting for your apology. The length of the silent treatment often means that the punishment does not fit the perceived crime. Once the child or person

"ME. ME, ME"
An inside look into the fragile heart of a self-absorbed mother

(NPD's do this in all their relationships) contacts them and either apologises or tries to rebuild the relationship then it reinforces the narcissists inflated view of herself. It also gives them a great sense of power and control and they will then use that control to bite back putting you 'firmly in your place.'

They particularly use the silent if you use assertiveness towards the NPD, confront their behaviour or refuse to meet their demands.

> IF I CUT YOU OFF ITS BECAUSE YOU HANDED ME THE SCISSORS.

The silent treatment effectually cuts you off and sends the clear message that you are insignificant in their lives and that they can clearly live without you. This then becomes a learned behaviour for the narcissist mother's child. As adults they may too use the silent treatment as a way of punishing people who have upset or angered them.

However those children that develop healthy ways of dealing with interpersonal relationship difficulties and make contact with the NPD parent hoping to sort things out in a constructive way or those who display an emotional response to

"ME. ME, ME"
An inside look into the fragile heart of a self-absorbed mother

the silent treatment BEWARE! It will be like jumping into a shark infested sea covered in blood. The NPD parent will see this as a weakness and as like a shark one sniff of blood they will jump on you and go in for the kill.

The best solution is to roll your eyes, sigh and show that it has no effect and once they see that this form of punishment is no longer effective then hopefully they will stop using it, unless of course you value the respite from the narcissist.

Hoovering is the term used for the narcissists attempt to bring an 'escaped' victim back into the fold in order to resume feeding the narcissist.

A hoover is a metaphor taken from the popular brand of vacuum cleaners and refers to how a narcissist can 'suck you back in' whenever they need their fix.

It is likely to happen when mum is not getting her fix from the other siblings within the family or her friends. She may use hovering when her own self worth is feeling particularly low and she is not getting her narcissistic supply. This is a time when the NPD may apologise (although be mindful that it will not be genuine), or may offer the child gifts, compliments or promises. They may tell the child how much they have missed them being in their life.

They may begin hovering when they are feeling alone or are ill and need additional supply. It may be when they need to be cared for and to feel loved.

For the adult child it will feel good all their 'need to be loved' by this person buttons will be pressed. They may develop

"ME. ME, ME"
An inside look into the fragile heart of a self-absorbed mother

the belief that their mother has changed and they are indeed significant to them after all.

It is important to remember that the NPD mother may have an ulterior motive. NPD's are adept at knowing what words to say, what gifts to buy that will draw their child in, after all they have known them all their lives. However that does not mean that she is not being sincere. Whilst they are hovering they may not consciously be trying to manipulate you. Be mindful that mum may not be conscious of what or why she is doing this, just that she is in some level of emotional pain. They may be convincing because **they** are convinced right now that they need you in their life.

Unfortunately you have to be the adult, maybe even parent in this relationship and take what she says with a pinch of salt, just like you would a child when they have magical thinking. Go back into the relationship (if that's what you want to do) with your eyes wide open, using the skills in this book.

Never-the less, keep your boundaries tight, don't give up any activities or relationships that you may have elsewhere. Be prepared that the 'silent treatment' may come again but don't fall back into old patterns of behaviour such as 'people pleasing' to prevent this from happening again.

The flying monkey is the term used for people who do the narcissists bidding, this would be to inflict additional torment or to simply spy on the victim or spread gossip.

If you have a narcissistic parent, you will definitely have flying monkeys in your life. Flying monkeys are people who

"ME. ME, ME"
An inside look into the fragile heart of a self-absorbed mother

take a part in the play that the narcissist parent is directing. Be mindful that the flying monkey will not have your best interests at heart because if they did they would refuse to step on to the NPD's stage or play the spy for the NPD.

They are willing and complicit partners although may have two different agendas.

Agenda One: They may be taking on the role of flying monkey to try and get reconciliation between you and the NPD parent. This may be a genuine act of kindness or they may want some respite for themselves as they are worn out by the NPD's behaviour. This flying monkey has probably been duped into helping and does the spying thinking that this will lead to reconciliation. This flying monkey may try to persuade you or guilt trip you into telling you your mother loves you and how much this separation is hurting her.

Agenda Two: They may not like you and so collude with the NPD in their vendetta against you. This flying monkey will believe all the lies that the NPD has told and will want you to pay. If this flying monkey is a narcissist then don't be surprised if you have vicious text messages or telephone calls.

Be mindful that none of the flying monkeys will be interested in or listen to your side of the story. They are just interested in their own agenda. None will have your best interests at heart. If they did they would not get pulled onto the stage.

"ME. ME, ME"
An inside look into the fragile heart of a self-absorbed mother

The flying monkey could be the golden child who will side with your mother to protect himself from becoming the black sheep or the scapegoat when out of awareness s/he is actually being the scapegoat because without a doubt the NPD mum will deny she ever asked the flying monkey to get involved in any spying or conflict or indeed reconciliation with you even when she has orchestrated the whole thing.

The flying monkey could be sneaky and ring you under the pretence that they are interested in you and your life. They may ask how things are and what is going on. Once they have this information they are straight on the phone to the NPD parent telling them all about your life.

The NPD also needs you to know everything about her life with her golden child, golden friends and golden family so she will use the 'flying monkeys' to pass this information on.

Some 'flying monkeys' could be being used, out of their conscious awareness and not be insightful enough to know that it's a narcissistic game, such as your children or your grandchildren.

They do all of this because even though you have been given the silent treatment they cannot bear not knowing everything about you and even worse they can't bear you not knowing anything about them and how well they are doing without you in their life, reinforcing your insignificance. They still need control. They want you back in their life to feed their narcissistic supply as they can never have enough feeders.

The flying monkeys are used to further their agenda, to feed their supply and to regain control.

"ME. ME, ME"
An inside look into the fragile heart of a self-absorbed mother

Flying monkeys can be people you have not heard from for years ringing out of the blue to check out how you are, you are so pleased to hear from this person that you eagerly tell them all about your life. Beware they will be reporting all of this back to the NPD.

So, the moral of this story is to be mindful and on your guard for the flying monkeys. They will come in all shapes, sizes and ages. Most of them will be prepared to do anything to further the narcissistic mother's agenda. They may do it out of awareness, out of loyalty to her or out of pure animosity towards you.

If a flying monkey comes your way be polite but tell them nothing of any importance and get away from them as soon as possible.

When a narcissist tells you a tale in which they are the innocent victim of some irrational monster... you are being recruited as a flying monkey.

Narcissistic Personality Disorder Mother on Facebook

"ME. ME, ME"
An inside look into the fragile heart of a self-absorbed mother

Chapter Ten
Will she change and how might I change - Contact or no contact?

One of the things we therapists say to our clients is that we can't change others; however what we can do is change ourselves which will inadvertently change the way people are towards us. In most cases this is the truth, but not with the narcissist. With narcissists when we change it stops feeding them and their needs. Our change can in many cases create more anxiety in them which subsequently results in more negative behavior.

Many theorists will say that people with NPD can never change and this is because they never see that they have done anything wrong so why would they need to change? What would they need to change they are perfect people?

Chances are that when you do start making changes and putting boundaries in place your mother's bad behavior may in fact escalate. The fact is that she may not change and I wouldn't like to give you hope that she will. However once you have an understanding of NPD and how little control that your mother has over her behavior it might help you to empathise and may

"ME. ME, ME"
An inside look into the fragile heart of a self-absorbed mother

release you of the anger and resentments that this has left you with. It may help you to maintain your relationship with your mother in a loving way.

Those NPD's that do go into therapy will do little work in the therapy room and will often report back to their loved ones that the therapist said there was nothing wrong with them and that they should indeed become therapists themselves. In fact they ended up helping the therapist sort out their problems.

Those that stay in therapy can become the therapists' worse nightmare. They will fight to keep a position of power, they will need to control the therapy session sticking to their own agendas. As in most therapeutic relationships the client will act out behaviour's in the therapy room as they do with significant others, so when the therapist begins to challenge their unhealthy behaviour's or take a peek at their 'real self' the NPD will be vindictive and angry towards the therapist. Their defenses will come up immediately to avoid going to that very painful place.

I believe that everyone has the ability to change, however with NPD's it would take long term psychodynamic or cognitive analytical therapy. To bring a narcissistic client to this type of awareness will be extremely painful for them. A client's defenses are there for a reason and a narcissist's defenses are rigid.

The best thing that you can do if you want to remain in contact with your narcissistic parent is to learn to accept her behaviour and accept that this is how she is. You won't change her, you won't be able to reason with her and whilst you spend half of your lives trying to do this you are not living your life. You are depleting your energy on a useless task.

"ME. ME, ME"
An inside look into the fragile heart of a self-absorbed mother

However, while you are accepting it and living your life try to keep your head together. Don't internalize her criticisms. Take everything she says with a pinch of salt. Accept that her reality is far from the truth. Don't give her the opportunity to use you as a scapegoat. Don't fight to become the 'golden child' it's not worth it, it's a short term fix and is never genuine, there is always an ulterior motive for putting you on this pedestal, to gain attention from others, to manipulate your siblings to do more for her and to manipulate you into continuing your people pleasing behavior.

If one or two of your siblings are permanently on the 'golden child' throne don't waste your time trying to get them to understand the psychopathology of your mum as they are often the last to realize there's a problem with her, if they ever do.

See mum as usual, just give up any hope of ever having a normal mother-daughter or mother-son relationship. Develop a good sense of humor and try to laugh at her often predictable behavior rather than becoming frustrated with her. She will try to draw you into her games, or stepping on to her stage, try to avoid this at all costs and at the risk of her rejection because believe me the game will be far more painful in the long term.

Also:

- Stop feeling guilty. Your narcissist mum will often try to use guilt as a way of manipulating you into doing what they need you to do.

"ME. ME, ME"
An inside look into the fragile heart of a self-absorbed mother

- Be assertive and say no without fearing rejection, rejection bites harder when you have 'done' lots of things that you didn't want to do, that you did to please and gain love.

- Put in place boundaries, what is acceptable for you and what is not? They will try to break those boundaries by creating dramas, tears or emergencies. Don't let them.

- Be mindful that they like to create dramas before special events or family occasions. Don't let them. Put things in place to stop this. If you have made plans to go out or go on holiday stick to those plans and don't let any self inflicted emergency halt your plans. Have someone on standby, another relative or close friend to fill your place if there is an emergency.

- Don't tell them anything that they may use at a later date to embarrass or humiliate you.

- Often NPD's will ring every day especially if they know your attention is being shared elsewhere i.e. your own children or partner. Unplug the cord when and if you need to, which is symbolically cutting the umbilical cord which they desperately want to remain attached to, under their terms.

- Be open and honest with other family members so that they can support you. You can share experiences so that they

"ME. ME, ME"
An inside look into the fragile heart of a self-absorbed mother

don't get manipulated into the NPD's drama and exaggerated stories about you, if you feel that they will be receptive to those discussions. Often children of NPD parents have a covert or overt message that they cannot criticize the parent. It's not criticism, it's a sharing of experiences about your mum, all children do this.

- If they have created a drama to grab your attention or told malicious stories about you, don't bite, even to ring up and yell at them is a source of energy for them and gives them attention.

- Let go of the useless hope that she might change.

- Don't share your confidences, NPD's are not good at keeping secrets especially if they feel that it will get them admired by the receiver. They may also use your confidences to cause trouble if they can. Provide information on a need to know basis, just because your NPD parent tells you everything often breaking people's confidences in the process doesn't mean you have to do the same.

- Shield your own children from the narcissistic grandparent. They do not need to be exposed to their toxic behaviors. This doesn't mean prevent them from seeing the NPD, it just means protecting them from becoming flying monkeys.

"ME. ME, ME"
An inside look into the fragile heart of a self-absorbed mother

- Accept that you can't change them. Accept that you don't have a 'gingerbread mum' and she can't help the way she is.

- Keep limited contact, the less you are involved the more you can stay out of the dramas. If a drama does evolve when you are around them don't step on the stage, leave.

- NPD's love to give advice and it is their way or no way. They are wounded if you don't take it. Rather than tell them that you do not want to hear their advice nor take it, which will leave them incredibly wounded and by now you will know how they act out when they feel wounded. Paraphrase or summarise the advice back to them and then do what you want anyway.

- Erase the belief that it is your job to fix things.

- Have plenty time out. Seek out a therapist that specializes in this area (some don't) to help you to come to terms with the affect this has had on you in the past, present and explore ways in which you can respond to this in the future.

- Don't let the NPD ruin or control your life or your relationships.

- As with a child when they are demanding attention at an inconvenient time tell them calmly and strongly "No I am

"ME, ME, ME"
An inside look into the fragile heart of a self-absorbed mother

unable to do that at the minute" In the same constructive way that you would speak to a child doing this.

- As they age don't take full responsibility for their care and don't let either the NPD or your siblings manipulate you into doing this.

Most of the reading you will find on the internet or in other books is to have no contact with the narcissist. However most of the reading is about having a narcissist partner. Occasionally you may come across this advice when it is a family member including your mother. I actually disagree with this if it is a family member, it is hard to turn away from your mother, she is the woman who gave birth to you and raised you after all and raised you in the best way that she knew how, and despite this disorder there will be many nice things that she has done for you.

Never the less what you need to do is separate yourself from the co-dependent relationship that you have with your mother, that is very often typical of the relationship between narcissistic parents and their children. Stop the need for validation from her; get it from the people in your life that will give it. Your contact needs to be measured and limited for your own peace of mind.

In chapter eleven I hope to give you some understanding of what is going on in the narcissists mind and heart and why they are not able to give you the love that you need. I hope that this helps you to develop some empathy for this lost soul and

"ME. ME, ME"
An inside look into the fragile heart of a self-absorbed mother

therefore work to maintain the relationship. After all she needs her family more than most. When narcissists are lonely they have to sit with no self worth, think of how painful that would be.

> Narcissistic parents abuse their children in many different ways. Some narcissists pretend to be "nice" occasionally, in an effort to keep the child hooked into the dysfunctional cycle. This has the child hoping and longing for acceptance from the parent...that never comes.

"ME. ME, ME"
An inside look into the fragile heart of a self-absorbed mother

Chapter Eleven
The Fragile Heart

For all the narcissist mother's confidence and presentation of specialness, inside she has a very poorly defined inner self. She is constantly plagued with feelings of inadequacy and not being good enough and this has been born from her own history. If you know your mums history then you may be able to make your own links, if you don't know then maybe this could be part of your journey to find out. A therapist will be able to help you to make sense of it all.

Your mum's need to be perfect is extremely powerful and when that perfectionism is challenged then the feelings underneath all of this are massively overwhelming.

Your mum is constantly disowning her imperfect unhealed parts of her self and projecting them on to others because to face them is one of her biggest fears. To face the fact that she is not this incredible being that she is pretending to be would leave her with feelings that are so painful which could become unmanageable for her. The more people that challenge her behaviours or try to force her to take responsibility for her behaviour, the more she will project this on to others as a form of a defence, which is a mechanism that most of us use as a

"ME. ME, ME"
An inside look into the fragile heart of a self-absorbed mother

protection. The narcissist however has such a deep and painful wound that the defences needed are much bigger than the rest of us.

When you confront the narcissist you are saying "here are your broken disowned parts" – the narcissist will automatically go into automatic deflection and projection.

The narcissist is so full of self disgust that to strip her of her 'perfect immaculate skin' would leave her to face the self hatred that she has for her real self. She has over her own childhood and adult life developed a 'false self' due to her own very low self esteem. It is therefore not surprising then that when she fears her real self coming out into the open that she then uses her necessary emotional survival mechanisms.

In the meantime even when there is peace in the family or her 'false self' is not being challenged mum may still have painful internal times when the unhealed parts of her, scream out painfully for attention. To stop this pain she will either do something to draw attention or adoration. This may be to try and get someone to do something for her **immediately** as a quick and immediate fix. Or create dramas as a form of distraction from her painful wound. In times when she is unable to do this she will throw herself into doing things such as housework, gardening etc. Her pain is extremely overwhelming so she will need to do physical things to avoid the pain, too avoid looking at her true self.

To help you to understand this you have to imagine that your mum has two 'self's' – her true self and her false self. She was born like most of us as her true self. However sometime in

"ME, ME, ME"
An inside look into the fragile heart of a self-absorbed mother

her own childhood something happened that was so painful for her which left her for some reason despising her 'true self.' It was then she developed her 'false self'. (For anyone who has studied multiple personality disorder you will find that it is similar. MPD's develop different personalities as a form of protection. It is a way for them to separate horrific experiences by devising a new chaste or tough personality. It is a way to disown aspects of their own character and their own perceived disgust at allowing this experience to happen to them). With NPD's they do not develop another personality they develop a 'false self' – a more likeable self, a more grandiose self.

The 'false self' is tough and can absorb any amount of pain, hurt and negative emotions. It is in a sense a gold cloak or suit of armour that they have wrapped around them to protect themselves. The gold cloak allows them to be anything they want to be other than who they really are, because who they believe they really are is so awful to them (to us it most likely wouldn't be) that it belongs in the bottom of the murky sea.

They have developed this 'gold cloak' to fend off hurt. It is so thick that it is almost impenetrable. The gold cloak is warm and cosy and makes the NPD feel exceptionally good. The 'true self' is so despised by the narcissist, so imperfect and in so much pain that lo and behold if anyone tries to strip them of their comforting and protective gold coat, their 'false self'. To strip them of their gold coat means that they will have to look at their 'true self.'

Whatever it was that happened to them, whatever they believe that they did in their past to create this experience or

"ME. ME, ME"
An inside look into the fragile heart of a self-absorbed mother

protect themselves feels so bad to them that they can't bear to face it. The narcissist despises the 'true self' for having failed to cope with the unrealistic demands and unexpected changes in their life. This can be a self blame for a parent leaving the family, something embarrassing they did in early childhood or early trauma or abuse.

The narcissist can be filled with toxic shame. Non narcissists can suffer with toxic shame too, clients who feel that they are so damaged, feel so helpless so filled with shame that they long to escape into a world of fantasy and become a completely different person. This is not too dissimilar to what a narcissist does. They are so unhappy with their 'true self' that they can frequently create fantasy 'self's' that feels a better place to be in.

Therapy would be able to reality test this with them, but their beliefs about the 'true self' which are so instilled in them, so strong, their pain so crushing that even a therapist would struggle to convince them that their true self is truly a good person. In fact some theorists will say that the reason a NPD does not commit suicide (although some will threaten to) is that they died a long time ago. There 'true self' is already deceased, disowned and no longer a part of them.

Does this mean that their feelings died with them? Which leads me on to, why can't narcissist's feel empathy, when so many people that have experienced traumatic childhoods have an overdose of empathy for other people whom have suffered?

There are many theories to this but I relate to the concept that other people in the NPD's life serve mainly to provide narcissistic supply which helps them to contain their shame.

"ME. ME, ME"
An inside look into the fragile heart of a self-absorbed mother

When people exist in our lives to fulfil a specific need then it is difficult to listen deeply to what it is like to live in their world. If someone is there to dump all their bad feelings on then why the heck would they want to feel what they are feeling because they would be partly responsible for the way this person is feeling and this would reinforce their feelings of shame.

Realistically if a person is there just as a commodity to admire and adore you and make you feel better about yourself would you really want to stop and walk in their shoes for a while to feel their bad feelings?

It is impossible for any of us to empathise with people we have no interest in. Although if this is the case is it more about the narcissist not wanting to empathise rather then not having the ability to?

I genuinely believe they can't. I feel that they have more than enough to cope with in their own feeling box to have the ability to feel what others are feeling. They are constantly striving to eliminate their own bad feelings to be able to genuinely step into the world of another being.

Also how can a 'false self' empathise? If you decide to be someone else for the day or week or even years how can you step out of character to step into someone else's world, when you are already stepping into someone else's world, a false character's world. To be able to really connect with another person you have to be your true congruent and transparent self.

I think NPD's do try to empathise and we misunderstand them. Notice when you tell your mum about an experience. What does she do? She tells you about an experience that she

"ME. ME, ME"
An inside look into the fragile heart of a self-absorbed mother

has had that is similar. Is this her trying to empathise? Does she have to revisit a similar experience of her own to feel her feelings to help her to understand yours? Is that her attempt at empathy?

My hypothesis is that when she discounts your feelings or makes comments such as "pull your socks up" or "I can't cope with this right now" or distances herself off from you, which then leaves you feeling invalidated is because she is everlastingly trying to manage her own.

From my research and professional experience I have come to the conclusion that if a client wants a relationship with their mum, narcissist or not it's really about accepting their mum's limitations. She is who she is and she is who she is because of her life experiences. She does her best with limited resources, no different from a mother who is disabled.

Her projections on to others are because she is unable to manage her excruciating pain of who she really is. She is a very unhappy soul and if she has to project even the behaviours of her 'false self' too then she can't like her 'false self' much either.

They have very little or no self esteem and feel that they have to pretend to be something they are not to increase their self esteem. They are unable to feel loved and accepted unless they are seen as perfect. They spend their life being phoney because they are unable to be their real self. They do not have the capacity to feel an intense love for others. They are not able to love and nurture their 'true self'. They have to plan day after day ways in which they can get attention and their narcissistic supply filled to enable them to survive another day without

"ME. ME, ME"
An inside look into the fragile heart of a self-absorbed mother

excruciating emotional pain and toxic shame. They cannot accept or hear about any negative behaviour because it would just resurrect that toxic shame. Due to this they are not able to grow on an emotional level. (Feedback given constructively facilitates our emotional growth). Every day is about survival.

For me it feels like they are blind and live a life without colour, they are deaf and live a life without music, they are made of stone so live a life without touch. They have no other senses so live a life without taste and live a life without the fragrant smell of the changing seasons. All of which requires us to stop and live in the here and now, which is impossible for a mother who is unable to sit with the stillness of life.

If they are unable to empathise then that does not mean that we can't. We thankfully are able to step into their world and feel what they are feeling and what it must be like to feel a void, emptiness, a nothingness. What it is like to have such a deep sense of self hatred. What it must be like to have to pretend we are, what we are not, to be accepted. What it must be like not to be able to empathise or love on an intense level. What it must be like to carry around such a painful wound and not be able to talk about it and that is even if they can consciously name it. We can understand their 'gold coat' and why they desperately need to wear it to protect that wound, that is so, so painful.

How can we not feel something for someone who despite all of this gave birth to the child, took a risk and offered that child a life, something that they conceivably lost many years ago. That in itself takes strength.

"ME. ME, ME"
An inside look into the fragile heart of a self-absorbed mother

Raising a child as best you can with a visible and cognisant disability is difficult in itself, but imagine raising a child with an invisible problem. A problem you 'feel' but have no conscious awareness of why you feel the way you do. Raising a child where you know on a certain level that you are undermining them, treating them in a unhealthy way but you can't stop yourself because to stop yourself would mean sitting with an intensity of pain that would leave you dysfunctional.

I believe that to a certain extent narcissistic mothers do love their children, if they didn't then they wouldn't feed them, clothe them, keep them warm, and well provided for. Their love is just hindered by the behaviours, by the gold coat that they have to wear to survive.

> **There comes a day when you realise that turning the page is the best feeling in the world, because you realise there is much more to the book than the page you were stuck on.**

"ME. ME, ME"
An inside look into the fragile heart of a self-absorbed mother

Chapter Twelve
Healing the huge wound

Healing from such a traumatic and sometimes cleverly hidden childhood is a daunting task. The child has had their own emotional needs unmet for so long that the notion of recovery may seem impossible.

When something is missing from your life (and this also applies for people when they have one or two absent parents too), it creates a vacuum, a hole that is so big and painful we try desperately throughout our life and our relationships for that wound to be healed, for that hole to be filled. The fact of the matter is that only the person who left it there in the first place can fill it in the time that they were meant to fill it.

As children of narcissistic parents that is near on impossible because the narcissistic parent will deny, distort and discount the fact that they did anything wrong or untoward in the first place. Never the less this is why as adults we continue to people please both the NPD parent and significant others in our life. This is why we continue to rescue the NPD parent and put their needs and the needs of others before ourselves. This is why we suppress our feelings; try so hard to be good and perfect. This is

"ME. ME, ME"
An inside look into the fragile heart of a self-absorbed mother

also why we fear being assertive, independence and love. We are forever trying to fill that hole or avoid the rejection and abandonment that has been the result in having our own thoughts, feelings and independence.

We believe that if we continue on our old ways then one day we will feel accepted and loved and the painful throbbing heart of our empty wound will heal. It won't! It will only set us up for further rejection and abandonment and make that wound bigger.

We need to learn to heal ourselves, and to do that we need to access therapy with a practitioner that has experience and knowledge around personality disorders. However here are some guidelines to help you towards recovery from the wounds left by a narcissistic mother. Please don't try to do this all in one go, you will need to take one step at a time:

- Gain an understanding of NPD by reading. This will help you to develop awareness that this is not your fault. That you are not and never were responsible for your mother's feelings or anyone else's. You will also learn to recognise the common manipulation tactics of a person with NPD. This subsequently will help you to put a name on what has happened to you as a child and as an adult making it less effective on you in the future.

- Begin to accept that your mum had NPD through no fault of her own.

"ME. ME, ME"
An inside look into the fragile heart of a self-absorbed mother

- Begin working through the grieving process, and the stages of grief – allow yourself to grieve the parent you never had.

- Acknowledge that you have never learned how to properly deal with feelings and allow yourself to experience those feelings.

- Work towards loving that inner child in ways that your narcissistic parent never did.

- Stop hoping that a narcissistic parent will change and begin to fill that hole, heal that pain. She will **not** change. Release that feeling of toxic hope.

- Psychologically separate from your mother.

- Get in touch with yourself who you are and who you want to be.

- Get in touch with and process the trauma and overwhelming feelings that are remnants of your difficult childhood. There is a difference between intellectually processing and feeling the 'feelings.' You will need to feel those feelings not continue to emotionally detach and intellectually process. Allow yourself to feel the feeling associated with the memory.

"ME. ME, ME"
An inside look into the fragile heart of a self-absorbed mother

- Work through the suppressed anger. Start by reading some anger management material and learn to express your anger in a constructive way.

- Remind yourself on a daily basis that you need to take care of yourself, that your needs are just as important as everyone else's.

- Do some reading on improving your self esteem and confidence.

- Stop being afraid of her or afraid of upsetting her. You are an adult and your life is now your own.

- When a narcissist is accusing you or labelling you and projecting their behaviour, thoughts and feelings on to you remember that she is talking to a mirror. Try not to internalise the tirade and allow it to affect your own self worth.

- Accept that nothing you do for her will be enough, just as quick as you became the golden child, you can become the black sheep that has done nothing for her. This is her stuff. Take away the power that she has to label you.

- Begin to love yourself for who you are **not** what you can do for others.

"ME. ME, ME"
An inside look into the fragile heart of a self-absorbed mother

- Get rid of the feeling of not fitting in or belonging. Be accepting of yourself and who you are. We are not alone and that includes you.

- Accept that you are an adult now and the only person that you have to please is yourself.

- Learn to be more autonomous, make decisions for yourself as you are the driver of your own bus.

- Learn to discount, ignore or self talk your own feelings of guilt and shame that the NPD parent has left you with.

- Accept that your needs are important so don't be afraid to make them known and ask for what you need.

- Accept that 'everything is **not** your fault and stop taking responsibility for everyone's mistakes, usually to protect them.

- Accept that you cannot rescue every situation to avoid conflict or histrionics.

- Learn how to be empathic with your own significant others to prevent the next generation from suffering in the same way.

- Get comfortable with silence and the silent treatment.

"ME. ME, ME"
An inside look into the fragile heart of a self-absorbed mother

- Learn how to be yourself and not what you believe everyone else wants you to be including your mother.

- Start to get to know yourself better and accept yourself. Shed that false image of yourself that has been projected on to you. You have spent a lot of time and energy focussed on the narcissist that you may not even know who you are or what you enjoy. Learn about yourself.

- Accept that you are not being selfish by taking care of yourself and getting your needs met.

- Learn to set healthy boundaries and assert yourself in healthy ways in your relationships.

- Learn how to trust people that are blatantly genuine in your life. Taking baby steps at first and then taking bigger steps.

- Don't suffer in silence if you are upset accept that it is okay and healthy to say that you are upset.

- Be careful about attracting any more unhealthy relationships. Start to build reciprocal relationships. One way to learn to differentiate between friends and frienemies is if the person makes you feel good about yourself then this person is a genuine friend. If when you

"ME. ME, ME"
An inside look into the fragile heart of a self-absorbed mother

are in their company it decreases your self esteem then they are likely to be frienemies.

- Make sure you get good sleep. Sleep helps you to recover and make good decisions about your life.

- Learn to have fun without the fear of disapproval.

- Be mindful of your responses to others such as rescuing behaviours, minimising unacceptable behaviour, people pleasing etc to ensure that you are not a magnet for other people with NPD.

- Develop a good routine of self care.

You do have the ability to heal and enjoy your life happily and healthily. Be mindful that how you were treated as a child and subsequently as an adult is not your fault, **but** it is now your responsibility to make choices for yourself.

"ME. ME, ME"
An inside look into the fragile heart of a self-absorbed mother

Chapter Thirteen

Coming to terms with life with a mum who is different & moving forward

I hope that now you have gained an understanding of the traits and behaviours of the narcissist, that you can now empathise with her fragile heart and that you can now move forward into maintaining a relationship with her.

It is painful for anyone to be estranged from their family and no less painful for the NPD. Even though she may be demonstrating how insignificant you are in her life, how she does not need you, this is just her survival mechanism. This is not what is in her fragile heart. The words she cannot say in a genuine way due to her own fear of rejection and a massive blow to her already damaged self esteem are "I love you and miss you and so want you to be in my life."

I experience that before a NPD survivor can go through this they need to go through four stages:

Stage One: Understanding of the narcissist and why she does what she does.

"ME. ME, ME"
An inside look into the fragile heart of a self-absorbed mother

Stage Two: Acceptance: accepting that you have a mum that is unable to show you the love that other mums do, acceptance that she does love you in her own way with the limited resources that she has, acceptance that she is unable to empathise with you or put you before herself, acceptance that she has no control over her sometimes difficult behaviours.

Stage Three: Grief: You will need to grieve for all that you have lost, all that you have never had and will never have.

Stage Four: Empathy for all that she has endured and her inability to feel in the same way as you and others.

I hope that this book has enabled you to start the process. Once you have gone through these stages then you will be able to develop a healthy relationship with her. However to maintain that relationship you will need to do the following:

- Wear a golden cloak to protect your own feelings when your mum does or says something that upsets you.

- Have someone close that understands what is going on that you can process your feelings with if they become to overwhelming.

- Stop internalising the blame that she may throw at you. Remind yourself that there is something wrong with your mum not you.

"ME. ME, ME"
An inside look into the fragile heart of a self-absorbed mother

- Stop trying to please her to gain her love. This will subsequently prevent the resentment and anger.

- Don't get pulled into the manipulation tactics of self and others.

- Meet your own needs and wants before Mum's.

- Enjoy plenty of activities outside of the relationship with your mum.

- Release yourself of the chains that once tied you to her by accepting that you are not going to get what you want. Get those needs met from other relationships or in self care.

- Use humour and try and laugh at some of the narcissistic things she does when she is full of self entitlement.

- Don't put mum in charge of your self esteem (nor anyone else for that matter). Your self esteem belongs to you, so don't rely on others to lift it or crush it.

- Get in the habit of putting yourself first and following your dreams and goals.

- Avoid unnecessary conflict. Walk away. Write a letter to your mum and ceremoniously burn it rather than challenge her over something that she is unable to change.

"ME. ME, ME"
An inside look into the fragile heart of a self-absorbed mother

- Be assertive with mum using words such as "You are very special to me but I am unable to do that right now mum" and stick with it.

- Ignore the frowns of disapproval when you do this.

- If you get the silent treatment use this time as respite and enjoy.

- If she looks hurt, give her a hug and move on to another subject.

- Own your part in the relationship, you have responded, colluded with this behaviour over a long period of time. Now you want to change.

- Accept that one day you may be the Golden child the next the black sheep., avoid being the scapegoat

- Communicate with your siblings if you are able to, to get them to recognise and manage mums behaviour in a different way.

- Read self help and inspirational books that motivate you and give you strength.

- Spend time with people who love and support you.

"ME. ME, ME"
An inside look into the fragile heart of a self-absorbed mother

- Allow yourself to feel your feelings, you have most likely suppressed them for a very long time due to your mums inability to manage those feelings.

- Self talk, tell yourself how special and loved by other people you are.

- Internalise and accept the love from others. If you are constantly searching and finding ways to gain the love of your mother you will fail to spot the love of others.

- If things get difficult limit your time with your mum. If you have siblings share the time you spend with her.

- If you are on the receiving end of a snippy, clipped, semi silent treatment, you can say something like "Mum, I love you and I want our relationship to be enjoyable and supportive, however when you give me the silent treatment it damages our relationship. I am going to end this conversation now but look forward to speaking to you when you can speak to me openly without giving me the silent treatment"

- Accept your mum for who she is and not who you would like her to be.

- Be grateful that you are not walking in her shoes and that you have the ability to love deeply and empathise with others.

"ME. ME, ME"
An inside look into the fragile heart of a self-absorbed mother

I know if may seem unfair that it is you that has to make all these changes, but a NPD does not have the same ability as you to change. It will be far more painful for her and she may not see that she needs to change. In the long run those changes will help you to manage the relationship and keep you safe.

> IF YOU'RE GOING HOME TO AN UNSUPPORTIVE FAMILY THIS HOLIDAY SEASON, REMEMBER THAT YOUR WORTH IS NOT DEFINED BY WHAT THEY SAY OR HOW THEY TREAT YOU.

"ME. ME, ME"
An inside look into the fragile heart of a self-absorbed mother

Epilogue

Narcissistic personality disorder is a diagnosed mental illness and can only be diagnosed by a psychiatrist or mental health practitioner who has trained in personality disorders. Children of 'narcissistic parents' do not have the experience or knowledge to make that diagnosis, however they do have the experience of their mother to recognise symptoms of narcissism. It depends on where their mother is located on the narcissistic spectrum as to if she just has slight narcissistic tendencies to full blown narcissistic personality disorder.

NPD is a mental illness and is often something that you cannot see or touch. It is like an invisible disability and very often goes undiagnosed and subsequently untreated.

As with many disabilities including mental health many children become the carers within the family unit. With NPD this is no different, often there is a role reversal with this illness whereby the child becomes the parent and the parent becomes the child. This may be because mum is the needy one, it may be a deeper issue and link to a lack of attachment that the mother had with her own mother. It may be linked to childhood trauma or indeed genetic.

"ME. ME, ME"
An inside look into the fragile heart of a self-absorbed mother

Never-the-less children with narcissistic parents may consciously or unconsciously live with and look after a parent with this hidden and secretive mental illness.

It is estimated that there are 10,000 to 40,000 young carers in the UK of which about one third care for a mentally ill parent. This figure would possibly be much higher if NPD's were amongst the figures.

Young carers are something of a "hidden problem" being either unknown to services or being left to cope. A study by the NSPCC showed that many young carers had significant experiences of loss, self blame and stigma.

Parental mental illness can significantly impact on family life and children are especially vulnerable. Compared with adults, children have more limited coping skills and strategies. They are more dependent on other people in their lives and have fewer psychological defences.

The greatest risk to the majority of children is not one of physical safety but of risk to their own attachments & development. They often miss out on educational, social and leisure activities.

Mental health research now shows that young people are particularly vulnerable to psychiatric problems, as are the children of psychotic parents.

Families often have little knowledge of their loved ones mental illness and find it difficult to know where to turn to get information. Without that information families can become very pessimistic about the future.

"ME. ME, ME"
An inside look into the fragile heart of a self-absorbed mother

It is imperative that family members find sources of information that help them to understand how the illness affects the person.

They need to know that with medication, psychotherapy or a combination of both, the majority of people do return to a normal life style.

It is also imperative that the family finds sources of support for themselves.

In both cases clergy, mental health and social services can play a critical role in identifying resources in the community that can help the family build the knowledge base that will give them the tools to assist their loved one and themselves.

Currently psychotherapy in specialised areas within mental health is limited. There is a lot of help for people suffering with mild to severe depression, anxiety and trauma related issues within mental health services today.

However when it comes to personality disorders, childhood abuse, and severe mental health problems that do not fit into this category, there appears to be a lack of resources and long term psychotherapy services, and therefore long waiting lists in areas where there is help.

I hope, as do many therapists and mental health staffs, to see an improvement in this area in the future, hope for children who are in awareness or out of awareness caring for parents who have severe mental health issues. I would personally like to see help for children whose own developmental needs are greatly affected to ensure that their own futures are healthy ones.

"ME. ME, ME"
An inside look into the fragile heart of a self-absorbed mother

Last but not least I sincerely hope that those reading this book both survivors and therapists have found it to be beneficial to their growth as I did researching and writing it.

Trust in your inner self, the love of your inner parent and the love of the people that surround you.

Best Wishes

Linda Mather

"ME, ME, ME"
An inside look into the fragile heart of a self-absorbed mother

> Mirror, mirror on the wall, who's the biggest fool of all? It must be the girl who can't stop crying. Or maybe it's the girl who kept on trying.

"ME. ME, ME"
An inside look into the fragile heart of a self-absorbed mother

Other Books by Linda Mather

"ME. ME, ME"
An inside look into the fragile heart of a self-absorbed mother

Introduction to counselling skills and theory ideal for students starting their counselling journey – Introduction and Level 2 certificate.

Manual for students studying Level 3 & 4 counselling skills and theory.

Self help books by Linda Mather.

This is a self help book for everyone's emotional growth. It explores the masks we develop through our lives, how we get them, why and how to get rid of them to facilitate healthy relationships, healthy lifestyle and see the world through fresh eyes.

"ME. ME, ME"
An inside look into the fragile heart of a self-absorbed mother

This is a self help book for people who are suffering with depression. It explores the causes of depression and includes tools to help people to manage their depression.

This is a self help book and a reference book for people who are suffering with addiction and for those working in addiction. It includes several tools to facilitate recovery.

This is a tool to help parents through their children's teenage years. It includes tools and humor to help us to manage this difficult stage, and the forever changing relationship.

"ME. ME, ME"
An inside look into the fragile heart of a self-absorbed mother

Novels by this Author:

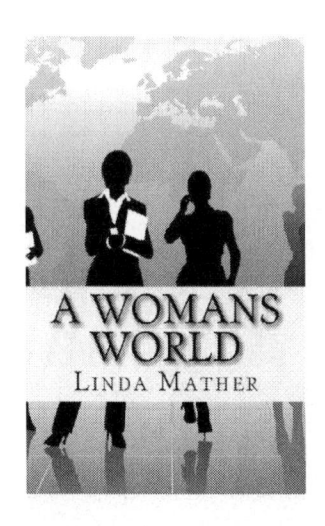

"ME. ME, ME"
An inside look into the fragile heart of a self-absorbed mother

Reviews for "Gut Instinct"

Mather has created an exciting and fast paced thrill ride. Her characters are sympathetic and believable. She adds several twists to keep the reader turning the page. As a mystery writer myself, I expect a good deal from an author in this genre. Mather delivers. Because of her professional background, Mather is a master of the Psychological Thriller. Her keen insight into human nature and her ability to surprise the reader, make this novel a must read for mystery fans. I look forward to more works from this first time novelist.

Ali Roberti - Author of NEVERMORE

Brilliant!!!,

I was engrossed right from the start. Excellent piece of writing, keeps you hanging on the whole way through! I love psychological thrillers; this is one of the best I have read in a long time! What an ending, well done, the author fantastic read!!!!

Twisted tale!

"ME. ME, ME"
An inside look into the fragile heart of a self-absorbed mother

I was sucked into the story early on and spent the rest of the day reading. Easy to read, amusing, puzzling, sad, savage, insightful AND with a twist in the tale. I am looking forward to the next book.

Brillant
Well I didn't expect that at the end. I couldn't put this book down and read 30 chapters in one night. Well done on a brilliant book.

Excellent!
This is an excellent read, the author has the style of James Patterson and although a slow beginning a page turner four chapters in.

Brilliant Read!
I could not put this book down it should be turned into a film. What an ending!!!

Mindboggling!
This book is an incredible psychological thriller that has you gripped from beginning to end, and what an ending. This author is a wonderful storyteller. I would recommend it to anyone who likes thrillers to read this

Great book!
I read this book in two days, considering if I can't get into a book within the first two chapters I don't read it, I would say

"ME. ME, ME"
An inside look into the fragile heart of a self-absorbed mother

that it says a lot for this book. Very well written, good story. Would recommend it. Well done Linda Mather. I can't wait to read the next one going to download it now.

Wow!!

All I can say is wow! What a fantastic book. I loved how the chapters changed between the story itself and the killers thoughts. Great read, would definitely recommend! A lot of research clearly went in to this book.

Excellent!

Enjoyed very much didn't work out the killer so that was a welcome change. I hope to read more of her books

Enjoyed

Worth reading for plot and the complication of the story. Not what I expected and you can relate to characters emotions

Reviews for "A woman's world"

A thought provoking book.

"ME. ME, ME"
An inside look into the fragile heart of a self-absorbed mother

Another great book! This author has the ability to get you thinking even after you have finished the book.

Food for thought
Would the grass be greener? Would the world be a better place? This is a story that gives us insights into the alternatives and asks us 'Which world would you prefer to live in?' Linda's second novel is as easy to read as the first and just as enjoyable. I suspect the film would have plenty of scope for some interesting details.

Good Storyteller
I am impressed with your story telling abilities.

Thought provoking
This is an interesting concept; this writer has a good way of telling stories, a thought provoking book. A thoroughly enjoyable read.

Reviews for "Jane, me and myself"

"ME. ME, ME"
An inside look into the fragile heart of a self-absorbed mother

Engrossing!

This is her best book yet, the clinical knowledge, the flow of the story and the way in which I was able to visualize each of the characters. The highs and lows of emotions; I experienced them all. I believe that this author does indeed grow with each of her publications and I look forward to many more.

Brilliant!

Just finished reading Jane, me and myself written by a local author, I thought gut instinct was good but this was even better. It was very well written and a brilliant twist at the end.

Brilliant.

Yet again a fantastic book, was gripped from the very start and enjoyed the twist at the end. well done to this author on another brill book.

Fantastic Read

I loved the twists that came along during reading this book. I do hope that the author writes many more books like this one and Gut Instinct. Both books are very hard to put down once you start reading them. Tell the house work it can wait while you sit and enjoy these two books. Well done Linda can we have some more please.

Thought provoking!

A very good read, I didn't see the twist coming at all. Thank you for such a poignant story about mental health issues.

"ME. ME, ME"
An inside look into the fragile heart of a self-absorbed mother

Children's books by this Author:

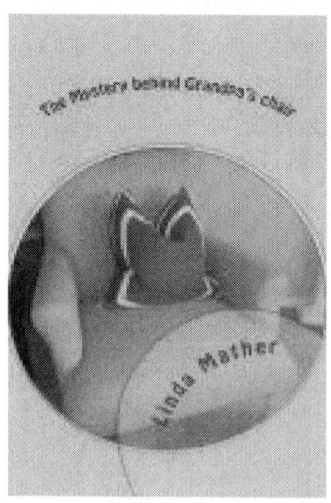

All available on Amazon or Barnes and Nobel

"ME, ME, ME"
An inside look into the fragile heart of a self-absorbed mother

Recommended reading

What's the message?
By Helen Stewart and Simon Carnell

A helpful book for managing challenging behaviour, for parents and professionals

"ME. ME, ME"
An inside look into the fragile heart of a self-absorbed mother

Printed in Great Britain
by Amazon